FROM THE MOB TO THE

THERAPIST'S CHAIR

DR. MONTY WEINSTEIN
WRITTEN BY: VICKIE TAYLOR

Family Therapy Center for New York & Georgia, Inc.

This is a personalized account of the life of Dr. Myron "Monty" Weinstein. Names, characters, organizations, places and events of Dr. Monty's patients have been changed to protect their confidences, unless they have specifically offered permission for their use.

Dr. Monty Weinstein | Vickie Taylor
www.familyunity.com

This book is dedicated to my beautiful wife and children
who have been and continue to be the most precious part of my life.

Table of Contents

Chapter 1

GROWING UP...

I was born August 2, 1939, as Meyer Greenberg. My biological father, Bill Abel, named me after Meyer Lansky, a notable Jewish mafia warlord who was brought to fame in the movie the Godfather.

We lived in a beautiful home situated on Manhattan Beach, a residential, upper class area at that time in Brooklyn, New York. My home was 40 feet away from the Atlantic Ocean, and 60 years ago in the 1950s, it was a private, residential area.

I remember, even though it was so many years ago, several strange things happening to me as a child. My mother, who according to my childhood memories seemed to always be in the process of getting a divorce, spent a great deal of her time selling precious diamonds to mafia warlords in Manhattan and its suburbs.

Some of her clients were Luciano and Anastasia and members of reputable Italian families. *"They'll probably kill me after I write this, but what the hell. I've had a good life,"* *I can't help but think.*

I remember at a very young age having a step-father. He was a doctor and a Colonel in the US Army. It is from him where I got the surname that I use today. Dr. Joseph Weinstein was a cardiologist in the Army in World War II. I was just a young, curious boy. My mother and stepfather changed my name from Greenberg to Weinstein. They didn't want me to bear the stigma of being affiliated with a mafia family.

I was born during a time when the Jews were being slaughtered in Germany. World War II was underway, and I remember some of the good things my family did. The military was very important to my step-father. I remember vividly our family hosting many, many hungry, exhausted sailors from the US Naval Base during the war. The Naval Base was adjacent to my home. We provided the sailors with shelter, a home-cooked meal, and a safe, clean place to rest. I enjoyed hanging out with them, listening to their stories. They were kind to me, probably closer to my age than my parents' ages. Perhaps I reminded them of their younger siblings, helped them in some small way with their home sickness. They were protecting our freedoms. Our Country – the Great USA – was not fully aware at that point of the horrors that Hitler was accomplishing across Europe at that time.

Somewhere around 1942 or 1943, I remember, if I may use psychobabble terms, feeling scared and traumatized when thugs tried to kidnap my 8-year-old sister. Another "gift" of being associated with the mob, I suspect. My sister, Roberta Greenberg, who was five years older than me, was kidnapped on the way home from school one afternoon. I remember that a car pulled up next to her as she was walking home from school, and someone jumped out and grabbed her, yanking her inside the vehicle.

Fortunately for Roberta, the family that lived across the street from us was outside and saw it all happening.

And this was not a small family.

Witnessing the crime take place were five robust, Italian boys all around Roberta's age and older who regularly played outside with her. When they realized what was transpiring, they chased after the car on foot and were able to break a car window to get the car to stop. They got Roberta out of the car. The car sped off, but not before a couple of those boys got some quick jabs in.

This was a traumatic event for me and Roberta. There was much speculation by family and local law enforcement that the car had stopped, and its driver or passengers had lured Roberta in with candy or something to get her to talk to them. I vaguely remember the police at my house taking a report about the incident.

Roberta suffered from anxiety and a lot of mental health issues throughout her short life, and I believe this incident was a precipitating factor. Our neighborhood boys undoubtedly saved my sister's life.

Ironically, my grandfather did not see it that way.

The fallout of this near tragedy as I remember it was that my biological grandfather, a powerful diamond dealer from Vienna, yelled crossly in outrage and blamed my sister.

Remember she was 8 at that time. He blamed her. He told her she had provoked it somehow, and she was the ultimate cause of it happening.

Rumors started flying. Several people talked. Some said it was a vendetta by "certain groups" against my father.

The term Mafia was not freely spoken at that time, and we did not discuss it in our home.

In my heart I wanted to believe that my family meant well, but it was basically, totally dysfunctional.

My early life was total chaos and confusion, and I think I developed a deep love for black, nurturing women as a result of my nanny, who was hired by my family to take care of me. Even as a child, I remember thinking abstractly and sort of blaming myself for the conflict between my mother and father. My father, William Greenberg, alias Bill Abel, spent a healthy portion of my childhood and much of his adult lifetime enjoying free stays at the county jail.

When he was not locked up, he ran a successful garment business that was located in what is known today as Rockefeller Center in New York City.

In an attempt to shield me from some of the ups and downs at home, my family shipped me and my sister off to Palm Beach where we spent many weeks at a time with our beloved nanny. Our nanny became the steadfast, parental figure to whom Roberta and I clung. She watched us as we played in and out of the ocean, on the beach in the sand building castles. We took what felt like hundreds of pictures that our nanny would dutifully send to my father. She was safe for us, and we loved her.

I have many memories of my beautiful, great grandmother, Frieda Rosenfeld, with whom I also spent a lengthy portion of my childhood. She, too, was a wonderful, warm, nurturing person. She was full of spirit, and very loving and devoted to her grandchildren. She was my maternal grandfather's mother.

As a youth, I remember frequently being in trouble. Grandma Frieda was already in her 70s or 80s. She would cook for me, buy me baseball bats, and always consoled me when I got into fist fights or got into trouble ditching school.

My mother would go ballistic.

My grandmother was always there, taking my side, trying to calm my Mother. Grandma Frieda was from Russia. She was a very beautiful woman. She loved to cook, and made the most spectacular cheesecakes. I wished I could have spent more time with her.

Instead, Mother sent me off to Hebrew school.

And I hated it.

I was bored.

I would leave class early and take off to the theater down the street. I could see three cowboy movies for 5 cents. I quickly learned that this was a much better option than Hebrew school.

The cowboy movies were a good distraction from the dysfunction of my home life. I had what felt like never-ending, childhood chaos. I blamed myself for the insanity and break-up of my family.

Chapter 2

MISSING FATHER...

I knew at a very early age that somewhere I had a father, but the constant guilt and confusion of him disappearing during long periods of time majorly impacted me in later years. I did not see that man from the age of 3 to the age of 16 as he just disappeared. He completely fell off the grid as far as this family was concerned. My mother kept saying he was dating some mafia woman, whom I knew at that time only as "Delores" from the Chicago Syndicate. I met "Delores" later in life. She indeed left a lasting impression. She was always drunk when we went out to dinner. She was a professional singer at various nightclubs in New York, and I recall her sharing stories of her friendship with Frank Sinatra.

During my father's extended absence, my mother constantly made excuses for him not being around. She told me that my dad could not leave Delores or "the family" (I presumed she meant the Mafia family) would kill him. This was repeated to me numerous times whenever I would ask why my father did not come home.

Because of my father's less than stellar reputation, we had to move out of Manhattan Beach and to another area on the outskirts of Brooklyn. I remember at the age of 7 moving to a new home and absolutely hating it. I missed the ocean. I missed the beautiful homes, the neighborhood where I'd lived my whole life, and mostly, my friends.

I have no doubt that the beauty of our Manhattan Beach home instilled in me an appreciation for finer things at an early age, and I totally enjoyed and appreciated our home there.

I'm pretty sure that Mother introduced me to Yeshiva, a Hebrew School for Jews, at this time as an attempt to save me and to save herself. She was humiliated and embarrassed because Dad was running around publicly with Delores. My mother constantly struggled to cope with it all.

Mother was sure that Yeshiva would save me.

I started at 8 a.m. and was there until 6 p.m., starting when I was 8 or 9, and then in the summer, Mother sent me and Roberta to Palm Beach with Grandma or the nanny to keep us out of her hair and distracted. In my heart, I grew up constantly feeling like I was in the way. Mother was routinely finding places to ship us. I suspect my mother truly enjoyed that I was gone all day. She could say she was taking care of me, while at the same time, she never saw me except for a fleeting moment late at night when she returned home from whatever distractions had kept her away all day.

Chapter 3

Dɪsaster: YESHIVA SCHOOL

I started at an early age bucking the system. I would go into the school through the front door, and then climb out the back window and go to the movie house. Back in those days, I could go see movies all day long. I remember going to what was known to me as the Garden Theatre and watching the cowboy films all day for what felt like several weeks, but was really only until I got caught. One day, a policeman saw me sitting there, trying to be all-grown up at the ripe age of 9. I was smoking a cigarette.

The officer made me go with him to the police station. He demanded to know where my mother was. I explained to him how she didn't come home until late at night, and my father had disappeared, but was most likely in jail. I must have pulled at his heart strings as I remember this tall, nice policeman transform from the stern authoritarian to a big, gentle teddy bear.

He said he was going to take me home to my Mother, and not say anything bad about me because he understood why I liked those cowboy movies so much.

What was going through my mind in those early years was not only the feeling of being rejected, but also a deep feeling that there must be something better in the world for me. I had a great deal of trouble during those formative years, and I often found myself spending the bulk of my free time with young Italian gangs which were common along New Utrecht Avenue.

On a side note, New Utrecht Avenue during the late 1940s and 1950s divided the Jewish and the Italian sections from each other in New York City. I spent a lot of time getting into fights, being suspended from school, going back to school and repeating the cycle; My mother, when she came home, said the only resolve for me was to send me to reform school where they would straighten me out.

So off to reform school I was forced to go. During those formative years, I was resistant to following the rules. I needed an outlet for my physical aggression, and I discovered boxing like so many other kids during that era. I spent a great deal of time boxing and weight-lifting, and for the first time in my adolescence, I began to transform. I was converting my reputation from being ornery to being a hard-working, tough kid from Brooklyn.

My mindset as a child swayed between being totally obsessed with fear and happiness: The Happiness, I suspect, was a hope that things could get better and I could have a good time. The Fear was likely a total disconnection from everything around me.

Later in life, while studying to become a therapist – and I hate that word by the way – I started to understand how certain people who break from reality or have severe anxiety disorders, can only think in terms of their world. While I directed a schizophrenic unit at the state hospital in Florida twenty plus years ago, I had a deep understanding of people who were not only chemically imbalanced, but who were lost and not able to connect with their surroundings. At times, as a child, I felt these feelings. Years later, as a therapist, I was able to empathize and help people who not only had psychological disorders but who were totally disconnected from their realities.

HIGH SCHOOL FIGHTING...

My first year at the Utrecht High school was not the best, and I was suspended multiple times. Utrecht High School was primarily a high school made up ethnically of Italians, and it did not take long for my mother to see that I had taken up a new hobby there: Fighting.

My mother through her ingenuity and wisdom thought that the best thing that she could do for me was to send me to Erasmus High School, one of the oldest schools in the United States at that time.

That also was a disaster, and I found myself frequently getting suspended there as well, and having a great deal of difficulty trying to play nice with others. I had problems with authority, a huge chip on my shoulder, and I knew that for survival, I would have to get some form of an education.

It's interesting to note that I did meet some interesting personalities during my troubled stay at Erasmus, people who were not famous at that time, but who made a name for themselves: Barbara Streisand, singer and songwriter, was in my class and graduated about the same time as I did. I remember her being funny and jolly. Another person who came out of that school and later made a name for himself was Danny Kaye, now deceased, but who was a very successful actor, singer, dancer and comedian.

During the early 1940s, I was just a kid, and I recall how my mother attempted to regain her social standing and respectability after her stint with Bill Abel. She was briefly a mob wife. It was stature and standing in a certain society that she longed to have back.

Thankfully, Dr. Joseph Weinstein intervened in Mom's plans. She started dating Dr. Joseph Weinstein, and he eventually became my step-father.

My mother had finally added respectability to the family.

While I would hesitate to admit it when I was a young man, I can safely, at this junction of my life, with confidence say that Dr. Weinstein was a solid, decent guy. I suspect his biggest faults or hang-ups were a result of his childhood growing up as a Jew in the Deep South. In spite of relatively few small faults, Joseph Weinstein fought in World War II and became a Colonel. He was on Eisenhower's staff and assisted directly in liberating concentration camps in Poland.

I strongly identified with him. However, because of his own rigid, self-guarded life, he was a bit distant and similar to those Midwestern people you meet on airplanes. *Insert chuckle here.*

Once Joseph Weinstein joined the family, the family somehow got together around 1958 to 1962 and decided that the time had come: I needed to be educated. With the change of men in my mother's life, I morphed from mafia role model to retired colonel as my role model.

Dr. Joseph Weinstein was a cardiologist and a retired colonel in the US Army. He was a rule follower, extremely bright, educated, and a truly good guy. His influences in my life were absolutely life-changing.

It was time that I converted my mischievous, hooligan self into a studious, career-driven youth. For the first time in my life, I took some of my high school studies a bit more seriously. I questioned most of the thinking, especially involving government and governmental surroundings. I spent a great deal of time reading to myself and drawing my own conclusions about the world around me.

Later on, this reflection helped me to understand how people reacted and interacted with each other, but in my better moments, in later life, I started to understand why it was so important. He was my example to become a healthy, positive father.

Chapter 4

Dysfunction: My "Normal" Life

Notably, domestic violence formulated the core of my feelings about life as a result of my observations when I was two and three years old.

I could never forget seeing what my father did to my mother.

My father was involved with a great deal of unsavory characters through his gambling and "collecting funds" from nightclubs. Sadly, I watched him take his fists to my mother, beating her up in front of me on several occasions.

To this day, while I am in my 70s, I still vividly remember her terror, his anger. I can hear the slaps, see his fists punch her body, hear her cries. I feared for her life. I was just a young child, and I was hiding, traumatized, helpless, frightened. It is also important to note that during years of psychoanalytical training, I understood and studied extensively the concept of transference and counter-transference, and I dedicated much of my work on learning to not project my own inadequacies on people whom I dealt with in therapeutic intervention.

Mafia On-the-Job Training...

At the age of 17, during the summer of 1958 and right before I entered college, I was once again spending time with my father for the first time in 16 years, and he helped me get a job where I would go around and collect money for the mob from various nightclubs in New York City. Part of my summer job was to go in, speak to the owner who was usually on the payroll of the mob, and demand, **and say in a very nice way**, that my father had sent me.

I was often hopeful that they could give me the envelope after they had offered me the shrimp cocktail. I was admittedly a bit feisty, full of attitude, and seemed to transition into this job naturally.

My father had much confidence in my skills. So much, in fact that he gave me a .45 caliber pistol to carry around with me as I made my rounds.

Otherwise, he would be negligent, he said.

There was no question that the mere existence of the handgun influenced and impacted my summer job performance. Without question, when these various nightclub owners saw me, they immediately produced envelopes which I then gave to my father. I was intimidating grown men into doing what I wanted them to do, and I was still a teen-ager. It was a powerful rush, but ultimately, I became very unsatisfied.

I was reaching an age that despite my summer job success, I recognized that I was feeling rejected. My summer job was causing total strangers to fear me. It was a feeling that I realized I did not like. Was it my conscience?

I also had a growing resentment toward my father. I was feeling used at the request that I continue to "collect" for him, and I was ethically feeling very torn about this summer job.

I was becoming aware that I lacked affection for my father. On two occasions and only on two occasions (because I still feared him as well), I took $100 bills out of two envelopes. Without any remorse, I went to the Copacabana and the Latin Quarter and enjoyed myself with my girlfriends on my father's dime.

COLLEGE...

I entered college in 1958, and at first, it was overwhelming. My family insisted that if they were going to help, which they did marginally, I had better study business because just maybe my father could help me get a job and not be a little gangster around Brooklyn. This thinking was clearly flawed.

Fast forward to college, and I had strict marching orders that I was supposed to be taking a business curriculum. After a year of business, I found it to be boring and nothing short of disgusting. I was miserable. I continued reading numerous books on a variety of topics. I met a very interesting man at college who was a philosophy professor, and he pointed me in the direction of classical books. I was hooked. I started getting more confidence in myself and changed to a philosophy major.

One day some of my friends were sitting around our college dorm, and we got a little drunk. Those friends included Dr. Joe Barkan, who later was appointed by President Nixon to be the director of the U.S. Office of Civil Rights, and my dear friend, Arthur Vendetta.

For some reason that I will likely never understand, I decided it would be an excellent idea to have a campfire in the dorm room. There was a really big guy, a football player who was totally obnoxious. I burned some of his school books.

Then I got suspended.

I was suspended for six months, and at that time, for some reason, I had finally attracted my mother's attention. She insisted that I go into therapy.

These therapeutic sessions changed my life.

They possibly saved me from myself. And through therapy, I met an amazing therapist who in so many words explained to me that I was acting out a lot of childhood fantasies against authority. During my six months of sessions with this therapist, my attitude improved. I seemed to find a better equilibrium, and so I headed back to school.

When I went back to school, I roomed with Frank Cuda, who later became a prominent attorney in upstate New York, and again Arthur Vendetta, who later became director for educational planning for New York City. I spent a good deal of my time breaking up fights between these two Italians, who later became, as previously stated, very prominent in their own rights.

I spent four years studying philosophy, and became very interested in existentialism, and the concept of individuality, and people making their own decisions independent of governmental authority. I later furthered my studies and received a Master's Degree from St. John's University in New York, and a Master's in Public Affairs with a concentration in Clinical and International Administration in mental health, from New York University, Wagner Graduate School, and a Doctorate from Hattie Rosenthal School of Psychoanalysis. Every year for 30 years I attended continuing education and post doctorate educational seminars from Harvard.

Afterwards I realized that in order for me to become a therapist, I needed to acquire experiences working with a variety of people and groups. I still had a great deal of growing up to do, and I desperately needed to deal with the inner demons that had been haunting me since I was a child.

Chapter 5

Family Life Drove The Training...

It is important to know that part of my training was not only dealing with research and books, it was validating my early childhood experiences. My formal training consisted of much graduate work. I received a bachelor of art's degree from Ithaca College in philosophy. I went on to receive a master's of science degree from St. John's University in counseling and psychology; My second Master's Degree was a Master of Public Administration from New York University. I received my doctor of Psychology (Psy.D.) from Heed University, Hattie Rosenthal School of Psychoanalysis. And each year thereafter, I spent countless hours on refresher courses, domestic violence training, couples therapy, autism therapy. I have at least 1,000 hours at Harvard University, participating in seminars, continuing education and advanced studies. I also participated in hundreds of hours of seminars at the Ackerman Institute for the Family. To continue this career, you must not be afraid to continue to grow and develop your education as your life experiences should be forever evolving.

Through all of my ongoing, sometimes troubling life experiences, I had approximately 1,000 hours of my own psychoanalysis.

I supervised training for therapists while in Florida at the State Hospital. The real inner part of my soul and training was the psychological experiences in early childhood. Feelings of rejection and not seeing or knowing my father for 16 years prompted me later on in life to advocate for fathers. Through advocating for fathers, I realized that there was a need for assistance for mothers as well. Over time, it has become clear to me that my gifts and talents are best realized when I am working for the weaker team, the downtrodden, scape goats, and ultimately the ones who are alienated in the relationship.

However, the real advocacy in my life has been for children and their accessibility to both parents. When I found myself helping my patients, clients and adolescents in psychiatric facilities who were dealing with feelings of rejection, I understood what that meant not only from a therapeutic point of view, but also and probably more profoundly, from my earlier experiences.

I was all too aware of that deep feeling of anxiety when I didn't know what was happening in my dysfunctional family. I had learned to survive and navigate through a sense of angst, which I later began to fully and deeply understand as I went through various phases of seminars and my formal training. I was transforming.

I was becoming a therapist.

Chapter 6

THE PSYCHIATRIC EXPERIENCE

In 1980 I was clinical director of a residential treatment center, the Montanari Psychiatric Center in Florida. Initially I mainly worked with adolescents. However, after working there several years, I interviewed for a position with the government in the Department of Health and Rehabilitative Services as a psychiatric unit director. More than 100 people interviewed for this position, and I got the job to direct the psychiatric unit of schizophrenic patients and patients who were deemed criminally insane.

According to the search committee, I was the "perfect fit" because I had training not only in psychology but also in mental health administration.

I was responsible for the deliverance of mental health services for all patients in Dade, Broward, and Palm Beach counties in Florida. I was clinical director of the psychiatric unit, and then was appointed director of the Equal Employment Opportunity Group at the hospital.

This was the mid-1970s to mid- 1980s. I worked there for about 10 years, until the unfortunate de-institutionalization of the hospital occurred. Many of those poor patients wound up in the streets because of a group from corporate America that decided they did not want to keep psychiatric patients in residential treatment in Broward County.

While I believe patients should be treated and released as quickly and expeditiously as possible so that they can become independent and learn how to live on their own, it was and continues to be, in my opinion, very difficult for schizophrenic patients to ever live independently.

I learned more about psychiatric services in that position than from any training I had at any University, including post-doctoral training from Harvard.

At that time, I learned the importance of family therapy which was just a pioneer discipline in the 70s and 80s, with very few mental health practitioners understanding what it was all about.

Ultimately, there was (and continues to be) a recidivism rate for schizophrenic patients which was very high, so after these patients were released back to the families, and the families had no experience in schizophrenia, these poor souls wound up back in the hospital for extended stays.

The only way to lower the recidivism rates was to educate the family on how to deal with psychiatric disabilities. And so I started to get my on-the-job training in family therapy and learned first-hand the importance of this discipline. Family therapy not only dealt with individuals who were mentally ill, but also dealt with their entire families by teaching family how to interact and cope. By teaching the families methods and means to move forward, these patients would have a much better chance in the outside world.

I started psychotherapy groups with the staff, including psychiatrists. I started support groups with schizophrenic patients, and also with the individuals who were treating them, including the mental health staff. I sat every morning, being the clinical mentor in psychiatric interviews of new patients with a multi-disciplinary team of psychiatrists, psychologists, social workers. I helped bring in the few family therapists that we had as part of the team at the hospital.

All this, I believe, was beginning to work to help these disadvantaged patients. I was starting to see some success, but it was short lived. A management team showed up, and immediately went to work de-institutionalizing the hospital, and I was sent 500 miles up Florida to Tallahassee, where I became director of research. This was a disaster, if one can imagine, a New York Jew being sent to Tallahassee to do research at a state hospital which was adjacent to the Alabama border. But the experience was great. And so I moved on with my life.

Chapter 7

Kibbutz:

In the spring of 1961, I wanted to connect with my Jewish roots and so I spent a great deal of time studying about the State of Israel. I was finishing my degree in philosophy, and was planning on doing graduate work at St. John's University in New York. Also, I was following my interest in studying psychoanalysis, and from there, I moved to the Hattie Rosenthal School of Psychoanalysis where I finished my graduate degree.

I had the opportunity through the Israeli government to travel on scholarship to Israel. They assigned me to live in a Kibbutz. A Kibbutz can best be described as a communal settlement around the Israeli borders. I managed to get a friend of mine to go with me, the late Dr. Joel Barkan who was later appointed by President Nixon to be Director of the US Office of Civil Rights overseeing civil rights of the entire country. We both flew to Israel, very naïve and very young. At that time, we were on a jet-prop plane, and it took us 15 hours with one stop over in Italy. I landed in Israel in the middle of the pitch, black night.

We were picked up by Israeli soldiers and taken to Kibbutz Sasa, which became a strategic military camp protecting Israel from Lebanon.

I woke up the next morning to find myself on top of a mountain as I looked out my window, and it was breathtaking. I was speechless. I was able to see in the distance the mountains of Lebanon, surrounded by beautiful fields of peaches, bananas, and all types of tropical fruits. The first several nights we stayed in a tent approximately 1,500 feet up the mountain. There was no idle time. Our work day started at 5 a.m., and I was told I would be on work detail, picking oranges and apples, and then be part of a communal meeting where everyone participated in the development of the Kibbutz.

At that time, in the 60s, the Kibbutz was a self-governing body, and what the workers picked and produced on the farm belonged to the workers who had equal rights in setting up the work details, sharing in the money, and basically everyone had a vote in what was going to happen.

At night, I was called in and volunteered to be in a security patrol which was stationed adjacent to a Lebanese border. For protection, I was given a German Mouser, a bolt-action rifle that was produced for the Germans before World War II, and that had been given to Israel by the German government after World War II.

I went out one night and was told that if we saw any gorillas (their word for the enemy soldiers) coming over the border, we were to listen to our communal leader and take cover. This was a very strange experience, but this was one of many strange experiences that I had there.

I had never been a participant in a group such as this, and it was an experience that was at that time unbelievable and difficult to describe. I felt a sense of comradery by being a participant in this communal society.

Later on, from 1966 to 1969 after I received a degree in International Administration from New York University, I wrote about Israel, Immigration and the struggles of people entering a new land which I believe was given to them 5,000 years ago.

I met a number of Arabs since my Kibbutz experience. I believe I have always been very open- minded. I became very close friends with Arab workers who were allowed to live on the Kibbutz, and we spent many nights around the campfire talking about how we all came from the same place.

During my Kibbutz stay, one day I was called in to the director's office. I was kind of frightened because I had missed several work details just being a screw up – and I had asked and allowed my friends to sign in for me. I was braced for a lecture and who knows what punishment. Instead I was shocked to learn that I would be given a special pass to go to the Eichmann Trial in Jerusalem in 1961.

Eichmann was one of Hitler's major officers who had been in charge of the total annihilation of the Jewish people. The Israelis who were living in the kibbutz were transformed into very tough, hard core soldiers, the backbone of the Israeli Army. They became officers in all the wars that Israel had to endure.

With my assignment to attend the Eichmann trial, I was picked up early one morning in May, 1961, driven by Jeep with Israeli military officers all the way to Jerusalem. By my side was my friend, Joel Barkan. This was an unbelievable experience since the Israeli soldiers had traveled to another country in search of Eichmann, found him, and brought him back to Israel to stand trial for his crimes.

Eichmann was charged with the annihilation of the Jewish people in the Concentration Camps. I will never forget. I listened to five days of him stating and repeating that he was only following orders. He must have said it 1,000 times. All of these atrocities happened to the Jewish people, but he was only following orders.

He was also charged with being a major participant in the annihilation of 20 million Russians.

I saw this man, sitting about 20 feet in front of me, in a glass cage, and I could not believe that such atrocities occurred, and finally, he was being brought to justice, facing a trial, which those poor innocent people never received during the Nazi atrocities.

Eichmann was later hung, even though Israel does not believe in capital punishment, but the government made special exception for him.

I do not believe, as a philosopher, that people can commit atrocities, without the support and aid of other people, and not too many years later, I was a participant with a wonderful group when I lived in Western Germany.

Chapter 8

THE EUROPEAN EXPERIENCE

Coming back to all these international and world experiences, I decided I wanted to study philosophy in Germany and was accepted to the University of Heidelberg by their philosophy department. One day while I was drinking beer *which is something they do there for a living apparently*, and speaking and talking about philosophy, I was recruited into the Deutsche Entwicklungsdienst.

The Deutsche Entwicklungsdienst offered German Aid to under-developed countries. I declined the studies at the University of Heidelberg, and moved forward with Entwicklungsdienst.

After some initial training, I was sent to be an educational and cultural coordinator to Waechtersbach, Germany. At that time, I was in my late 20s and I was given a suite at the Waechtersbach Castle.

I lived at the Castle which was like the set of a surrealistic movie, and I became very involved and immersed in the German culture.

I worked with German nationals, training them how to work with the various volunteers as well as their paid employees who belonged to this group and whose main goal was to provide informative seminars on recruiting more volunteers and employees. This organization sends volunteers into third-world countries, abroad, and worldwide to places in need, working somewhat like our Job Corps.

I became very close friends with a gentleman by the name of Henner Hess who later became a famous professor of sociology at the University of Berlin. Hess wrote about the mafia's influence throughout Europe.

I also fell in love. Her name was Ursula, and her father was one of the top CEOs at that time of Mercedes. Within six months, I found myself living with Ursula in one of her family's homes in the Black Forest. We spent close to a year riding around Europe, talking philosophy and living in paradise. This was the perfect type of living if you don't have to work, and at that time, I had already received a good deal of money for working with the German government.

One day, I was called by my boss to meet him at 4 a.m. by the Berlin Wall. I had a special pass, and I went into East Berlin with orders to report back about what was happening there. I had to report all of the happenings to authorities. I went through the wall, walked around, met a contact there and spent the next several weeks working in a psychiatric clinic in East Berlin. The communist section of Germany was severely depressing, and I stood out like a sore thumb being a crazy, Brooklyn Jew who somehow lived in a castle, was dating a prominent family's daughter, and was now in East Berlin "spying" for the non-communist sector.

These are some of the many experiences that gave me a totally upside-down version of what was going on in the world, but helped me gain a deeper insight into my surroundings including the crisis of 9-11 at the World Trade Center in 2001.

My German experience was short-lived. When my Jewish family caught wind in New York of what was happening in Germany, suffice it to say they were not pleased. They accused me of running off with a German woman, which was completely true at that time.

They did not hesitate to remind me of the irony of my situation. I was Jewish, living in Germany, where a few years earlier, my step-father had assisted in freeing Jewish concentration camps. I was disgracing the family, they said.

They threatened to cut me off financially if I did not immediately return home. I was young, naïve, and still completely, financially dependent on them. For whatever reason, after an amazing six more months in Germany and an empty bag of excuses as to why I just needed one more month, I sheepishly jumped on a plane and headed back to New York without looking back.

Chapter 9

REBOUNDING FOR LOVE: MARRIAGE WOES

While I was lovesick for Ursula for what felt like years, she remained in Germany. I was back in New York, and I had to move on with my life for the good of my family, I was told. I found myself living in Greenwich Village.

 It was here that I met my first wife, Ashira.

Ashira was totally and completely beautiful. She was Israeli. She had offers to model for Life Magazine, to be on their front cover. We were married for nine years. We each had hurdles to overcome, and neither of us was able to change enough to make the marriage last.

I had my own dysfunctional family hang-ups, and she was not used to American culture as she was raised in Israel.

The marriage fizzled in New York.

It is important to note that she came from a very wealthy family in Israel. Even so, as is common for Israelis, she returned to Israel after our divorce and became a member of the armed forces, and ultimately became a master sergeant in the Israeli Tank Corps.

I always tried to figure out why this marriage failed as I aged and reflected, and understood life a bit better. It is the insecurities in life and the challenge to overcome them that make life worth living.

From this marriage, I had two children, Alan and Lemore, whom I love very much to this day. Their mother and I were involved in a custodial dispute, and now that I look back on it, it was a totally devastating time for me in my life.

Ashira fell in love with someone else during our marriage and asked me for the divorce. This was extremely difficult to comprehend.

I felt betrayed, lonely, and protective of my two children. Yet, in the end, even though I was heart-broken beyond words, I had to move forward.

My son, Major Alan Weinstein of the United States Army Medical Corps, fought with US Forces in Iraq and served as a combat surgeon. He was commended by the younger President Bush in April, 2007, at the National Training Center with the Meritorious Service Award for his service in Iraq. He was part of the Stryker Brigade. Dr. Weinstein works today as an obstetrician. He is married to a beautiful, talented oncologist: Dr. Karen Weinstein who also fearlessly defended our country. She served in the United States Army Medical Corps along with Alan, was a national swimming champion at Ohio State, and has her board certifications, fellowship and doctorate in oncology.

My daughter Lemore is a very successful business woman with her husband Shawn. They hosted the International Domestic Violence Forum in Palm Beach. Lemore has a graduate degree from New York University's Wagner's School of Public Affairs in Public Administration. They have three beautiful children.

About eight years later, I met my second wife, Julia, a strong, Italian woman, and I was with her also for nine years. We had one daughter, Jacqueline. When Julia and I divorced, we were living in Florida. She wanted to go back to New York. She had a daughter from another marriage, Leticia. I literally raised Leticia. She attended Harvard, and I am very proud of her success.

Since Julia had returned to New York, I thought I should follow. I arrived, however, at roughly the same time as Julia filed for divorce.

In my heart, I believe that Julia meant well, but she could not stand living in Florida and wanted to move back to her Italian neighborhood in New York, where she and her family had settled from southern Italy. Whatever I might say about Julia, she was a good mother, and she deeply loved our daughter.

She just could not stand the pace of life in which I was involved. She felt more comfortable in her Benson Hurst home, and so we forged through some really heavy conflicts. We shared joint custody.

We had verbal wars back and forth for what felt like years, but at the end of the day with both of our moral support, Jacqueline was raised happily and is wildly successful. Today she is a children's oncologist and was previously a surgeon at the National Children's Hospital in Washington D.C. Jacqueline married Dr. Michael O'Neil, an emergency room physician. Jacqueline is currently working as an ear, nose and throat cancer surgeon for children at University of California, San Francisco. Both Jacqueline and her husband have dedicated their lives to helping those in need.

It is the essence of my life as I now reflect that every one of my life's experiences have transformed me and aided me in becoming the therapist that I am today.

I have endured a lifetime of conflict resolution and it has completely transformed me and my ability to understand people. Much of my expertise came from being out on the streets for long periods of time. That was my "on-the-job training."

One of the interesting factors about divorce and courts and custody and attorneys that I took away from my own experience as well as the hundreds of cases in which I have been involved, is that if you don't hate your spouse before the divorce, after dealing with matrimonial attorneys, sadly, you will.

Chapter 10

TURNING POINT

While I attempted to recover from my second divorce, pick up the pieces of my life, and find my place in the world, I was also continuing to struggle with relationship woes with my father. I was attempting to settle into a new, single life in Florida. During that time, my biological father came to visit. He was 80 years old and still in pretty good shape, but he drank a great deal. I'm sure his liver was pickled.

He bought a beautiful multi-million dollar condo on beach-front property, along the inter-coastal waterway in Miami. He was going to be living closer to me so we could have some quality time together, he said.

Keep in mind that my father was a feared, prominent member of the Mob, and as such, he was connected to a few unsavory people.

He accumulated his millions through night clubs, gambling and investments in buildings. He was a former fighter and an outstanding gambler, and a "selective" alcoholic, only drinking top-shelf liquors like black-labeled scotches. I recall that he finished at least two bottles of scotch nearly every time we met.

We were planning to meet for dinner one evening in Miami.

Instead, I received a call that he had been hit by a bus.

I was told afterwards by some of his friends, that he was murdered, intentionally pushed in front of the bus in Miami.

I soon received a call one day from his accountant that I would be a multi-millionaire because my father had buildings all over New York City. I spent three, long, turbulent years being the heir-apparent of my father's estate, along with my sister, Roberta.

Roberta also had children and grandchildren, one who was in a play on Broadway.

Then Roberta was found dead in a hotel. She was young. She was a good-natured soul who went to pieces when our father's estate was stolen from us. She was on my side, and we were both fighting for the inheritance.

Roberta married well, and the inheritance was not a major focus of her life. Her husband was wealthy, and before her life fell apart with the news of the death of our father, she and her family had lived happily in Patchogue, NY.

Unbeknownst to many people, Roberta lived just three blocks away from Adolph Hitler's brother. It was not common knowledge at the time that Hitler's brother was living in America, right under everyone's noses. If people knew, no one spoke about it. World War II was winding down. People were trying to get on with their lives.

Roberta and I were gearing up for a head-first plunge into the court system.

Initially, we were told that our father had no will. We were his only surviving children. He was not married at the time of his death. The estate should have been ours.

However, before Roberta and I knew what was happening, multiple versions of Bill Abel's *alleged* will surfaced.

I went to Court representing myself, and was immediately successful in being appointed Power of Attorney. On the surface, it appeared that my sister and I were the natural heirs to the estimated $20 million estate.

I should have known that this battle would not be so easy.

I was in my 50s, and I found myself in the middle of fighting some very influential people for my natural rights to the inheritance. How hard could it be?

One of the buildings owned by my father at the time of his death was a little, two-bedroom apartment a couple blocks from what today is known as Trump Towers. This little two-bedroom apartment is valued at more than $3 million in today's market.

Because of my stupidity, naivety, and otherwise irrational behavior at that time, I remained in contact with some of my longtime family friends and cousins who were living at that time in Sicily, Italy.

Those family members, as it turned out, had also remained close friends with my "cousins" and were working both sides of this inheritance squabble. They later relocated from Italy to Cherry Hill, New Jersey, most likely with the help of my father's dime.

I was asking questions and doing the legwork, and ultimately doing a lot of investigating to determine where my father's money could have been stashed. I suspected the bulk of his money was unreported given his non-traditional business ventures.

In Court, my beloved "Cousins" produced another document showing my Uncle was an heir.

I was devastated to find out that the "family" in Italy to whom I had been entrusting my confidences, was reporting all of my leads to my uncle, my father's brother, and cousins. I was doing the legwork and gathering facts, and it was all coming full-circle to be used against me.

Truthfully, I should have known I was playing with fire, and I was out of my league. It was my Uncle Jacamo, a Sicilian mobster, who flipped on me, becoming a trader against me. I was helping him with his own court battles, entrusting him with family secrets that he then shared with my father's brother. In Court, I continued to battle family. It was my Uncle's children who were attorneys in the US Senator D'Amato's office. They were the ones who were fighting against me, and I was handling my probate case on my own, pro se, against the Titanic. I did not win that fight for what was rightfully my inheritance. The battles lasted for what felt like years, until I finally realized that the stakes were simply too high.

According to some of my extended family members, there was a plan in motion to eliminate me. I tried to laugh it off as being too extreme, too violent, but when I learned that my uncle was building an extra room in his multi-million dollar estate, I became concerned.

Rumors were floating that the room was for my daughter, Lemore. I would learn years later from multiple extended family sources that my "beloved" uncle planned to take me out of the picture to remove me as a threat from inheriting my father's wealth.

Yet because of my uncle's upstanding sense of honor, he was going to raise Lemore as his own. When these rumors reached me, and I started to fully understand what was at stake and whom I was dealing with, I withdrew completely from that side of the family.

I had some form of education which was eye-opening for my understanding of my "family," and rather than pursue my father's millions, I decided I would help other people who came from dysfunctional families. I think my insight into human thought grew deeper as I became exposed to my own demons, my early childhood trauma, and my various experiences growing up.

Chapter 11

THE THERAPEUTIC WORLD...

It is accurate to say that several different events in my life motivated me to become a therapist and aid and assist people going through difficult times.

One of the cases, Smith v. Smith, involved a man who was in jail for racketeering and other mischievous deeds that land people in federal prison. He spent five years in a cage for his crimes. I learned of him through another mutual friend whom I was working for at the time as a trial consultant. My friend was undergoing a divorce and was plagued with various child-custody disputes. My friend was a devoted father who just wanted equal time with his children and after a torturous fight, became very involved in the parents' rights movement. Every time I saw him on the weekends, he would offer some crazy, convoluted story about his good friend Smith who was serving this federal prison sentence. He visited Smith regularly. Every weekend after his visits with Smith at the federal prison, he would share yet another story of Smith's predicament. He shared that his friend Smith had married into a very wealthy family that developed computers and various mechanical devices and hardware. He was extremely wealthy, yet he did deserve to serve that sentence for his crimes.

He took his punishment, and when he got out, he deserved to have a relationship with his children.

When Smith got out of prison, he came to visit me. He wanted my assistance gaining joint custody of his three children. I had a soft spot for him. After several conferences with him, I realized we experienced very similar childhoods. I felt in my therapeutic encounters, a bonded relationship with him as he began sharing details and struggles of his youth. He, too, grew up with an absentee father.

Smith was extremely bright and for whatever reason, we deeply identified with each other. I told him that even though he spent five years in prison I would help him navigate the system in order to get parenting time with his children. He had three beautiful children, and he lived in a $7 million mansion on the water.

Various attorneys told me to stay away from this case as Smith was organized crime at its best.

For me, I imagine that meant Smith could have been my family. For whatever reason in my pathology, we became good friends. When I attended Court with Smith, the Court appointed me to see his children who were all attending a beautiful, private school, Our Lady of the Sea. As I spoke to the children's principals, they all stated that the children dearly missed their father, and they were well aware that he had been in prison. It was clear during my meetings with the children, they were not happy just living with their mother, and they deeply missed and yearned for their father.

I went into Court on a number of occasions with Smith, and on this particular occasion, Smith didn't have a lawyer and was worried about not having one. I told him that he didn't need a lawyer, and I could help him through the hearing. Together we faced four different attorneys who were defending Smith's wife. Mrs. Smith basically was a very intelligent woman, but she was very entangled with the dark side. She was also connected to various sundry mafia groups.

It was during my time helping Smith that I met another lifelong friend and famous attorney who was known for cruising to Court in his Rolls Royce.

He was unforgettable. This is how Saul Edelstein entered my life.

During the Smith Case, the Court recognized that I was Smith's expert. We also brought in James Wilks who was, along with me, a co-founder of the National Association for Fathers. James was a very bright, brilliant, charismatic, civil rights leader who was formerly with the Black Panthers. James and I had been friends for numerous years.

Smith made a decision to believe in me, and instead of having a lawyer, he had a team of consultants that we hand-picked for their specialties. We all looked like we came out of central casting for the Sopranos. We had numerous Sicilians directly from Italy who came in and aided and assisted me during the whole trial which ultimately lasted several years.

Edelstein became very close to me as a result of the Smith case, and I spent numerous lunch hours speaking to him about life and getting to know his family.

I apologized profusely to Saul for the longevity of this case as it just went on and on, and I testified numerous times over the course of two years. It felt like, for me at least, the trial of the century in Stratton Island, New York.

At the end of the day, Smith wound up with joint custody of his children. As a result of our success, I received numerous new clients, coincidentally, several of them who had just gotten out of federal prison for various charges and who wanted my help getting visitation with their children.

The Smith case not only added the spark of new business to my life, but it also added several important connections to prominent professionals with whom I have now worked for several years.

Mr. Edelstein asked me to join him on a very interesting case that involved a major, successful, local attorney, Adam Roberts, who had initially lost his children during a custodial conflict in New York, and who was fighting to regain that custody. The prominent attorney's case consumed several months of our lives. I attended court some time later with Saul. I was representing as the client's therapeutic expert, and we were up against the wife's attorney, Dominic Barbra.

Barbra was notable for representing movie stars and the rich and famous. (Those were likely the only ones who could afford him.) I went into court on behalf of Roberts.

This case was unique and burned into my memory because on one occasion during a settlement conference, Saul and I accompanied our client to the law offices of Mr. Barbra. We were in the middle of the settlement conference when Farber ran out of his office and hollered for someone to call the police. He accused us of planting a bomb under Barbra's Rolls Royce. He charged that Saul's associates were actually planting the bomb, and he pointed his finger at me and claimed that I had engineered all of this.

No bomb was located under Barbra's car.

It was a rouse. Nothing was found. Total theatrics they were playing up. They were trying to smear our names, but it was fruitless.

It's important for me to note that I had not engineered this, nor would I ever do anything like this. I always had some form of respectability and professionalism even though I did have a different approach to dealing with the Court system.

My view of the court system was likely tainted from my upbringing as a son of a mobster, but ethically and morally, I remained bound to "doing the right thing."

As a result of working so closely with Mr. Roberts on his custodial dispute, I recruited him to assist me with the National Association for Parents. He became a very active member in the association for some period of time.

Now because of my tumultuous background, I also easily identified with this attorney. I liked him, and we worked well together. We spent much time together, but I started to notice that whenever we would meet, Mr. Roberts was becoming increasingly side-tracked and running out of the room to make phone calls on his cellular phone.

I chalked it up to his duties as a successful, prominent attorney.

I traveled with him to Georgia, where I was busy building my consulting business. After a year of working side by side with Roberts and spending countless hours with him, I could have never predicted his demise.

I was sitting in Killer Creek restaurant in Alpharetta, GA, and as I walked outside to get into Roberts' Mercedes, three FBI agents surrounded us and arrested him.

His arrest was in the NY Times, and was followed by a thorough investigation.

I was devastated to learn that my colleague was running a major gambling ring in the State of New York.

I later attended his jury trial. He was, at the time, the attorney for the National Association for Parents' Rights. Roberts was on the surface a good guy, and he joined the rest of the eccentric attorneys whom I had brought in to assist the National Association for Parents' Rights in New York.

Unfortunately, when he went to prison, his new digs put a damper on representing parents. I'm sure he helped many of his new-found friends in the federal prison. However, he was convicted, disbarred and sent away for five years for his misdeeds for laundering money for one of the five mafia families in New York. To this day, I would say that he was a very good friend of mine. I was his expert in his fight for equal parenting time with his children, and in my encounters with him, he always appeared to be a devoted father. I did not know anything about his side ventures.

I do not want to discredit Roberts. The facts speak for themselves. He fought hard for his clients. He was an excellent attorney, an excellent father, but he made some bad choices.

As long as I am on the kick of talking about attorneys who worked with me under my jurisdiction, I must address Robert Workman. He was another brilliant attorney whom I helped in a major custodial conflict where he was the litigant in New York. At the same time that he was the litigant, he was in therapy with me, and I must have seen him approximately 40 sessions.

One day I returned to my office in Greenwich Village where I never knew what famous folks I might pass along the way as it seemed to be a gathering place for famous people. I was reading the New York Times, and I found out that my patient, Workman, had been arrested for attempted murder. Workman at the time of his arrest worked as the law clerk to the chief matrimonial judge in the New York Supreme Court. Workman was fighting his own demons, and because of his personal conflict and instability, he stabbed the court clerk multiple times and was jailed.

I testified at his trial as his therapist, and as a result, the Judge demanded that I produce my psychotherapy records. This was at the time in front of a judge of Manhattan Supreme Court who later became the chief judge. He demanded that I produce all of my records of my confidential therapy with my patient.

I refused to do this as some of the therapeutic records disclosed private and possibly damning information about other people.

The Judge threatened to put me in jail for contempt.

I held firm and stated I would not produce the records, and if I was held in Contempt of Court and forced to attend a contempt hearing, it would have to be heard in front of a different judge. Ultimately I did not go to jail because they never held that hearing.

If they had forced me to go to court and produce those records, many of our local lawyers would have been in trouble. I won't say anything else about that.

At the same time, I was being pressured to give names of who was getting pay-offs because this was information that he may have had, but he could not disclose it.

Eventually, several of the named attorneys were indicted for various criminal activities, but that was not because of me. It was in my blood to never be a stool pigeon. Those deepest, darkest secrets will go with me to my grave.

Also, during this period of time I was much busier with work and new clients, receiving upwards of 40 calls daily from potential new clients who wanted me to either take on their case as an expert, assist them therapeutically or to help advocate on their behalf so they could regain custody of their children.

It was during this chaotic and hectic time, my first wife from whom I was divorced, was killed tragically in a car accident while picking up our daughter at the airport in Israel. I immediately regressed and felt the severe trauma. Even though she and I were involved in a difficult custody battle, the loss and shock was deeply devastating for me.

She was the mother of my children.

From that point forward I assumed the responsibility of raising my son who is now a doctor and former military officer, and my daughter Lemore who is a business administrator and happily married with her own three beautiful children.

I had to learn to live with and manage this severe trauma for many years. This tragedy ultimately helped me relate and personally understand some of the feelings of my patients who are down and out.

During this time, I became very close friends with Dr. Robert Gould who is a famous psychiatrist and professor of psychiatry at New York University and Columbia. We formed a partnership. He was the chairman of the Attica Prison in New York during the prison riots of September, 1971.

I also became good friends with Dr. Seth Farber, an extremely eccentric and brilliant psychologist who has written a number of books. At that time, I was asked also to make several television appearances and was on Matt Lauer, CBS, Channel 2, and was a guest for several years on a satellite television program, Children of Divorce, filmed at the top of the Empire State Building.

My career was really taking off. Yet, I was trying to cope with a number of things like the totally tragic situation of the death of my first wife. It was a very exciting yet very overwhelming, difficult time.

I was learning that being rich and famous did not protect folks from having their own skeletons in their closet.

Several famous people came to me for consultation and advice including movie actors and producers, a former astronaut, even a Disney Movie producer. Their cases were often times high-drama.

John Heard, the movie actor now deceased, used to hang out in my building, but I didn't know he was a movie star. I asked him more than once to go grab pizza for me. He didn't argue. He just went along his way and brought back pizza.

This little boy from Brooklyn was now testifying all over the country, was acquiring great respect, and soon would be traveling all over the world.

Chapter 12

Custodial Disputes Spanning the Atlantic:

Approximately 20 years after my Heidelberg, Germany experience, I was called to Constance, Germany to testify as an expert in a tragic custody battle on behalf of a father who was American born and his wife, who was German born, and who fled the United States and took their children to Germany. Mother was dealing with severe mental health issues.

Shortly after mother left the Country, father sought and was granted emergency custody orders out of Queens, New York. The basis was that Mother had basically kidnapped the children and relocated with them to Germany.

During this case, I flew to Germany with a colleague who was a retired colonel with the Green Berets and a major advocate for parents who had lost their children.

Mother stole the children from the State of New York, and we had a signed/ certified custody order out of New York granting father custody.

We soon learned that our Court Order was just a useless piece of paper in Germany.

I testified in an emergency hearing in Constance, Germany, a beautiful town on the Swiss border, on behalf of the American father in this case. The German Court refused to return the children to Father's care. They said our court order had no bearing on what they did or did not do.

We were allowed a have a home visit with the children before we left the country to ensure their safety. What I witnessed made me feel deep down that these children were being neglected. They were living inside a home with a foster parent who also owned 10 pit bulls, and all dogs and children were living inside the home. Their living environment was filthy, and yet, we were powerless to do anything but speak to the children briefly before leaving the country without those children.

I realized shortly after the visit that the Court was not complying with the Hague Convention since the father had custody, and the children therefore should have been returned to Father instead of being placed in foster care.

At that time, I was working as one of the executives for the National Association for Fathers, a national organization that had thousands of members not only throughout the United States but throughout Europe. I believed that since the German government was not complying with the New York State Court's order, and it was a member of the Hague Convention, that we should take the children across the border to Switzerland, and then fly them back to the States.

We toyed with the idea, but ultimately, it was the father's decision, and he did not want me to take that chance. As a result his children grew up in Germany with a foster-care parent while Mother spent time in and out of psychiatric institutions.

We did not want to become criminals even though our cause was righteous. We returned to New York without the children. This case ended disappointingly. We did what we could for our client, but it just wasn't enough.

A few years later, I received a call from the Washington Post when a reporter was doing an article on the Hague Convention and wanted to report some of the problems we were having with the German Government. I told my story. I do not know to this day if it was ever printed, but the father we tried to help went back to school, and to the best of my knowledge became an attorney trying to help people who were in similar situations.

Germany was a mixed bag, and after World War II, it was very difficult to get a full reading – a vibe on the feelings of older people who had lived through the war, especially for me since I was Jewish. The people from the younger generation, however, seemed to be very kind and warm, and my experience of being in Germany was totally positive. (In spite of my family thinking I was nuts to spend a year there).

Alaska...

A decade ago I was contacted by Rev. Pearson in the Kenai Peninsula of Alaska, stating that his son was having a very difficult time trying to see his children and trying to have a relationship with them.

They stated they wanted me to fly out to Alaska and assess the situation as Director for Mental Health for the National Association for Fathers.

Rev. Pearson, I found out when I arrived in Alaska, was the head of the Lutheran Church in that respective state. He flew me out and I met with him, his wife and his son. They were the salt of the earth, wonderful people.

I usually never stay at anyone's home, and I stayed at their home. I landed in Anchorage, and he took me over to view Mount McKinley, which was the highest mountain in North America at an elevation of 20,310 feet.

I flew in a three-seater plane from Anchorage to the Kenai Peninsula, going over the Yukon. I wound up approximately 25 miles from the Russian border, where according to Sarah Palin, former governor of Alaska and vice-presidential candidate, one could see Russia.

I don't recall seeing Russia.

The second day, the father and his son took me out to the edge of Alaska where I climbed on glaciers, slipping three times, but somehow managed to walk from one end of the glacier to another. There were several glaciers floating around there, it was cold, and the air was crisp.

Afterwards we prepared for Court, and after three trips to Alaska, I was able to testify before the Court on parental alienation.

The judge there was totally against this concept, and at the time thought it was totally radical. However, I was able to opine and make my statement, which I believe was totally correct in their situation. During my testimony, another person whom I thought I recognized but could not place at the time was sitting next to the ex-wife, aiding and assisting the lawyer at Counsel's table.

I later discovered that this person was a presiding judge from the state of Pennsylvania. To practice law in another state without a license was totally unbelievable and completely corrupt. When I got back, I received a call from the Philadelphia Enquirer, and they were going to do a major story on how a sitting judge from Philadelphia was practicing law in the state of Alaska. As the scandal was unfolding, I learned that the sitting judge who was assisting the ex-wife in Court was actually the paramour, the lover, of Mr. Pearson's ex-wife.

I wholeheartedly felt that this corruption should be made public. I waited anxiously for a major weekend story, hoping that this would get to the press, and that they would have the guts to publish it. However "someone" threatened to sue the Philadelphia Enquirer, and they never ran the story. These were just some of the anecdotes that I dealt with when I was aiding, assisting and advocating for fathers who were disenfranchised as a result of a court system that appeared to be biased and prejudiced.

COLORADO…

Several years ago, I had the opportunity to be called to Colorado on a case where they were going to terminate a Mother's parental rights. Her name was Cinnamon Welch. She lived in Aurora. She agreed to have her name used in this story. She was a very attractive, feisty woman who was married to a grouchy man who owned several car dealerships in Denver. He was extremely wealthy, and overly aggressive – which is why he was probably a natural for owning car dealerships. Cinnamon was basically a very nice, lively and spirited woman but she lacked aggressive tendencies like her husband.

She was losing the parental rights to her two children, ages 5 and 7, when she brought me in to help with her case. She also had another child whom she had raised alone since her prior husband had abandoned her. That child was 15 at the time.

Cinnamon's new husband was very hostile and violent, and had physically assaulted her on occasion.

Cinnamon's mouth did not help her. She was loud and sassy with a short fuse and all too often engaged in verbal altercations. By the time I arrived in Colorado, she no longer was allowed to care for her children. Yet when she detailed to me the process she had endured and how her children were removed from her care, it just felt like a total set up.

I consulted with a colleague, and he headed to Colorado to help me on this case. It was me and Peter Lomtevas, a brilliant New York attorney, and together we fought the system. We wound up suing the Adams County Department of Human Services in Federal Court. We followed our gut because we believed that particular county in Colorado was running a racquet. It appeared they were taking the children away from parents and receiving state funds. We challenged the Department of Human Services in Federal Court, and I wound up testifying on Cinnamon's behalf on five separate occasions. The Department said that Cinnamon had some major mental health issues. Based on my street smarts and not my psychological training, I realized the only issue that she had was that she was being too honest and her ability to express herself was flawed. She came very close to losing her children permanently, and after five major court hearings, we ended up on the winning side of the custody battle.

In another Colorado case I encountered one of the most extreme cases of parental alienation that I ever witnessed. A Colorado dairy farmer was divorced from his wife, a local veterinarian. They had three young children at the time I was brought in to the case.

Mother was of extreme intelligence, very controlling, and yet, ultimately, found to be struggling with mental illness. Father was a hard-working dairyman who just wanted a normal relationship with his children. He would have settled for an alternating weekend schedule with his children. However, Mother repeatedly blocked Father's visits, came up with "issues" that overlapped Father's parenting time. During parenting exchanges, Mother would hug and hold on to the children for up to an hour and a half, making Father wait and exclaiming that the children refused to leave her side. Mother scheduled activities during Father's summer parenting time. She told the children that Dad was stalking them, that they were not safe around him. She made random calls to local sheriff's deputies to do welfare checks on the children and she reported that she had received hang-up calls from the children and could hear screaming and crying in the background. With lights flashing and guns in hand, law enforcement showed up at Father's home during normal parenting time. They would find Father in the yard with his children, playing catch, riding bikes. One wrong move and father could have been shot by the deputies, who thought they were responding to some horrific altercation in which an out of control father was punishing his children.

These experiences traumatized the children and tainted Father's relationship with his children. It was alarming for them to see law enforcement show up in this manner.

On another occasion, Mother suggested, on the eve of Father taking the children camping in the mountains for the weekend, that the older children should not allow Father to be alone in the bathroom with their little brother, who was 3 at the time even though he still needed some assistance. The children were then terrified that Father was going to do something bad to their little brother. They said over and over that Father could not be left alone with the kids.

Year after year, when father was supposed to have extended holiday parenting time, Mother would come up with an excuse or an emergency why the children were unable to go with Father for the holiday or vacation time.

Father refused to give up even though it became apparent that he had an uphill battle. He hired child family investigators, parental rights evaluators, and finally, he hired the expert on parental alienation, Dr. Monty. After more than 10 years and hundreds of thousands of dollars in litigation and expert witness fees, Father was finally able to convince the Court, with my help, that Mother's behavior was alienating, damaging and emotionally harmful and detrimental to the children. She was clearly unable to foster a loving relationship between Father and the children.

Flash forward five more years, and the eldest son, 16 at the time, was so fed up with Mother's alienating behavior that he refused to return to Mother's home after a weekend visit with Father. He threatened to run away if Father made him return home.

Mother locked the child's dog in his crate, which was kept in the son's bedroom at Mother's house. She told her son she would not let the dog out until he came home. The son went to his mother's home to get his dog, and did find him in the crate, in his feces, because Mother refused to let the dog out.

Additionally, Mother reported a break in at her home after her son had returned to the home to get his beloved pet. Mother then filed an emergency motion to halt Father's visits and for the immediate return of the dog to her home.

Mother was asking her church congregation to pray over the children due to the "extreme abuse" they were suffering at the hands of their father, the children reported. The child was confused. He was experiencing a very different life at his Father's home. Father had remarried, had three more children, and their lives were going smoothly in comparison to the chaos at Mother's home.

After several more months of fighting, exhausting emergency hearings and an extensive therapeutic intervention, another doctor personally observed the eldest child's fear and ultimate refusal to even be in the same room as his Mother. At the mere suggestion that the child simply go visit Mother's home, the child declared he would run away. The doctor, after many meetings with the children, declared that the children should have no visits, absolutely zero contact with Mother, not even on a supervised basis, until Mother underwent extensive therapy.

My detailed explanation to the Court about parental alienation was pivotal in changing the dynamic of this case. The Court had previously said it would not remove Mother from the children's lives because her bond was stronger with the children as she had been the primary caregiver. No one could argue that Mother was the primary caregiver, as she had banished father from the children's lives and was becoming an expert at throwing up roadblocks whenever Father wanted time with the children. However, the tragedy for these children was that Father was denied long-term, the opportunity to be any kind of caregiver due to Mother's controlling and alienating behavior.

Pennsylvania:

In a case involving a client who became one of my dear friends, I was hired approximately seven to eight years ago to be the expert on parental alienation. His wife was refusing to allow him to have any contact with his children. Wife was demanding that Father undergo psychological evaluations, a number of them, and he was not testing well. He retained me to rebut the psychological evaluations of various doctors.

At some point throughout the process, I realized that the ex-wife suffered from a thinking disorder, and it was apparent from assessing the multiple psychological evaluations. I immediately realized that a thinking disorder is a delusional phenomenon, and it can reach to the level of a psychosis.

This was a beginning step for my client/ patient. However the court battle was lengthy and spanned several years before we were able to convince the right people to restore Dad's relationship with his beloved children.

Chapter 13

Meanwhile, in Georgia

Another case of extreme importance was a case with a gentleman by the name of Jim Dillon. Jim was an honest, straight-forward individual. His family was the picture of corporate America. He was extremely successful, doing everything right, and making a lot of money along the way.

Jim was an honest fellow who just wanted to be left alone to play country music at his lake house. He was married to his wife for 24 years, and they had six children. Jim played and conducted folk music at least 10 hours daily. While he was busy with his music, his wife had an affair, fell in love and wanted a divorce.

Although there were no prior allegations of violence, Jim's wife accused Jim of being abusive with their children. One by one, the children all came into court to testify against their father saying he was an abuser. The case started in Georgia where I assisted him and he successfully won his case at the Magistrate level. However, then the ex-wife relocated to Florida and started the case all over in Florida. She accused him of domestic violence. I was one of the individuals appointed to evaluate Jim, his ex-wife and all of the children.

Initially, all six children stated he was sexually abusive to them. My intuition was strong, and I smelled a rat. I had been out on the street, and my extensive experience working with families and children at that time did not lead me astray. I felt strongly that the children had been coached, and that their story was total bologna.

Several attorneys on Mother's side filed complaints against me stating that I was influencing the Court Evaluator, whom I knew from the past as we had taught seminars together.

Mother's attorneys also filed a complaint against the Court Evaluator who was one of the greatest diagnosticians I had ever met.

Ultimately, the Court threw out the complaints against both of us, and I testified that I firmly believed that the children were all coached and suffering from extreme alienation. Several years after the case concluded, all of the children came forward and stated they were told what to do by their then- therapist, and they are all now living with Jim Dillon, who has stayed in touch after all these years. He still sends me poetic folk music periodically.

I am enclosing some of the transcripts of a deposition where six attorneys deposed me for two days, and thanks to Peter Lomtevas' brilliant insight, we prevailed.

Chapter 14

FLORIDA

Part of my therapeutic training happened during my decade of living in Florida. During the 1970s, I had the opportunity to be trained at Jackson Memorial Hospital, Miami, where I became director of counseling for the first federally-funded methadone clinic in the country.

I spent hours upon hours learning the federal rules of detoxifying patients who were drug addicts. Because of my own insanity, I wound up running marathon groups which became popular in the early 70s, and consisted of all-night group sessions at the clinic with hard core drug addicts and felons.

I learned how to run groups successfully, efficiently, and how to deal with sociopathic behaviors and at the same time, I learned how to detoxify patients on drugs by substituting methadone. I realized after a while that the methadone had a similar affect as other drugs. However, to a degree, it stabilized patients. This was part of my role in becoming a therapist. I also worked in the 1970s as a director of the Montanari Residential Treatment Center, in Hialeah, Florida. It was one of the largest residential centers in the country.

Montanari and his connections with families in Boston ran a non-traditional act where he appointed me overall clinical administrator. Most of the time, he would go to Boston and I was responsible for running the center with close to 600 residents, children through adolescent-age. There were six psychiatrists and 12 psychologists who reported to me, and because of my training as a clinical administrator, I got Montanari accredited by the Joint Commission on Hospital Accreditation. I also worked as a psychiatric unit director in south Florida in Hollywood.

When I first came to that institution, we had thousands of patients, and I ran four units. One of the major hurdles for me was that I had custody of my four children and the clinic required a lot of time and attention.

After working in the clinical environment for 10 years successfully, a management team came in and de-institutionalized the hospital.

I was totally against this change, but no one listened to me.

I was sent to Tallahassee to be director of forensic research at Chattahoochee State Hospital.

FIGHTING THE SYSTEM

Part of my training in becoming a therapist was a combination of being on the street, being a member of gangs, and being exposed to various psychiatric facilities which institutionalized various patients. I was a psychiatric unit director for 10 years at South Florida State Hospital in Hollywood, Florida. I was in charge of six units and spent a decade observing patients in a multi-disciplinary role. I was responsible for approximately 200 patients at any given time. I was in charge of Dade, Broward, and Palm Beach counties. All of the patients who needed involuntary institutionalization were placed under my care. Part of my function was to administer a multi- disciplinary psychiatric team.

Every morning from 9 a.m. to noon I listened to psychotic patients tell their stories, and the team would vote on whether they would be institutionalized or sent back home. I sat with a board-certified psychiatrist, a clinical psychologist, a psychiatric social worker, and several mental health counselors. Every morning, we came up with a diagnosis predicated on the various behaviors of these patients. Most of these patients were schizophrenic, and there would be no university that could educate me more than the hands on, 10 years of working with patients who were psychotic.

I stayed there for 10 years and won several awards for my service, but then, because of a change in the political winds, the state decided to call in a management team for the sole purpose of de-institutionalizing the hospital.

I could not support this venture.

I firmly believed that patients who were severely psychotic were better off in a hospital setting rather than being thrown out to live on the streets.

My reward was that I was "relocated." The higher-ups sent me to Chattahoochee State Hospital, 500 miles down the road.

Being a New York Jew in Chattahoochee was similar to selling Hebrew National Hotdogs to the Third Reich.

The cultural experience was extreme.

However, I played nice with others, and I got through it. I had to get up every morning and take a bus with several psychiatrists to the Alabama border where the hospital was located.

I made some good friends despite the circumstances. One of the major problems was that I had custody at that time of my children, and I was not allowed to move them out of Dade and Broward counties, which were in South Florida. As a result, I filed a motion after spending a year as director of forensic planning at Chattahoochee, and was awarded the right to return to the South Florida State Hospital, which at that time had been reduced from 5,000 patients to 500.

I was made university liaison for licensing with the state, and I was given an office in the state prison. That stint did not last long. It was clear I was going batty. So I left that position, and decided to hang my own shingle.

I soon developed a practice which boomeranged out of control because the former psychiatrists with whom I had worked at Florida State Hospital were sending me referrals weekly. In no time, I became quite busy. My experience at the hospital gave me a much greater understanding of therapy and the role of a clinician.

Part of my evolvement in learning how to deal with people effectively was working out my own transference and counter-transference, and my own identity with all types of people. I had to transcend my own personal feelings towards people who were struggling and try to have some objectivity in order to get troubled people from point A to point B.

I understood that the insecurities in life and the challenge to overcome them was what it was all about.

Also, somewhere in my personal childhood experiences and my own ongoing, extensive psychoanalytical training, I finally understood that my self-worth was not dependent on what other people thought of me, but rather my own concept and my own feelings about myself.

One of the ways my life was formulated was when my father was murdered.

My father never really gave me any of the normal "fatherly" foundations or helped me navigate through early childhood. However, when he was run over by a bus, I felt a deep loss, and I understood that one of the subconsciously motivating factors later on, how I dealt with this trauma was assisting in the formation of Father's Rights Metro in New York.

Chapter 15

9-11: TERRORISM SURFACES IN OUR COUNTRY

The first day of my daughter Sophia's school was 9/11/2001.

I drove my daughter to her elementary school, and while I was driving I heard on the radio that the World Trade Center had been hit by accident by an airplane.

This was the first tower of the World Trade Center.

Five minutes later, I heard that the second tower at the World Trade Center had been hit.

And then I received numerous calls from friends and associates that I should turn on the television. The next thing I witnessed on the television was that the World Trade Centers were totally in flames. The towers of the original World Trade Center were only about five miles away from my home. I looked outside, and from Brooklyn I could see heavy smoke billowing out of the towers. Shortly after, I received a call from my son who said the Pentagon had also been attacked, that a plane crashed into it leaving a blaze of fire and dead bodies.

My son, Alan, who was an Army officer at the time, went to the World Trade Center to help recovery efforts. I received a call from the editor of the American Psychotherapy Journal who knew I lived in Brooklyn. He asked me what was going on, and I said I thought we were under attack. Weeks later, he asked me to do a column, bi-monthly, on terrorism and its psychological effects. I wrote that column from 2001 to 2009 and published 27 journal articles on terrorism, both internationally and domestically. My son Alan, because of his Army clearance, was allowed to go to the World Trade Center and help out as one of the responders.

I took a bus every morning to my office in Greenwich Village less than one-half mile away from the World Trade Center. I used to stop at the World Trade Center before arriving at my office in Greenwich Village.

I was saddened to learn that what seemed like half the people on my bus were killed, people with whom I spoke every day in simple conversations as all of us made our way through our daily routine.

The bombings did not discriminate against anyone.

It hit people from numerous nations, colors, religions, ethnic backgrounds, with the only commonality that they all worked in those beautiful towers.

This devastation to our country by terrorists had rippling affects throughout the world. Then President Bush arrived at the scene of the ashes of the World Trade Center and totally gave support to the people of New York, the nation, and the world. He especially praised the diligence and hard-work of the first responders and firemen. Shortly thereafter, my son and my daughter-in-law Major Alan Weinstein and Major Karen Weinstein were brought into active duty for the Army and my son was sent to Iraq.

He was commended years later by George W. Bush with admiration and respect. While I was not a Republican, I believed President Bush to be totally sincere in trying to avenge the more than 3,000 people who were annihilated in this cowardly act.

I was not thrilled that Alan was being sent to Iraq. However, he had special training and his skills were needed. He was one of the senior medical officers with the Stryker Brigade. Karen gave birth to my grandson on a military base which was part of the national training center in the United States. Alan, who is of slight build and about 5-feet, 8-inches tall was involved in helping wounded soldiers in Iraq. Alan was a rebel growing up, but his integration into the Army was a very positive, life-changing experience, and he received numerous commendations. I was and continue to be very proud of my son and daughter- in- law for their ongoing service to our country.

During this time, I struggled with a great deal of mixed emotions.

One does not really learn to be a mental health practitioner.

I firmly believe you either have it in you or you do not. And what I learned during these tumultuous years while our country was at war was that one cannot intellectually rationalize feelings and give it psychological labels.

One has to be integrated into the happenings around him or her and have compassion for people. I got involved in counseling veterans during these years, and I had many of them join the National Association for Fathers with me.

I got heavily involved in issues surrounding post-traumatic stress. I said to myself that this is the real thing because for the first time in the history of the United States we were attacked at home, our safety barriers were violated, and at the same time, I personally witnessed the horrors of airplanes full of innocent passengers slamming into the World Trade Center Towers. I smelled the smoke. I saw all of the ashes from the burning, collapsing buildings.

This horrific picture is forever stamped in my memory.

I felt that I must forge ahead to identify psychologically what allows people to commit such heinous and egregious crimes.

I started to write about this newly-discovered terror and received positive comments throughout the country. My next calling was trying to help numerous veterans who were contacting me for help with post-traumatic stress symptoms following the war.

Part of the severe anxiety that I felt was that once again, many of the people who were on the bus and who spoke to me in everyday conversations would no longer be going to the World Trade Center, and I wondered and obsessed how this was affecting their families.

This finally allowed me to find a sense of maturity that I had been striving for many years.

Chapter 16

Military Attempt:

If I were to flash back to 1958 when I was a freshman in college, I was still very much an adolescent, and many of my choices were kind of idiotic. My stint with the military got started on a dare while I was standing outside with several friends at the school.

I joined the Marines which were on that beautiful, sunny day in mid-October recruiting people for the platoon leader's class.

I bet my buddies $100 that I would join, and at 17 ½, I joined the Marines Officer Training Program.

At that time I was in incredible shape from boxing, weight-lifting and running. I made it all the way to the officers' training program. However, I arrived a week late to the training in Quantico, Virginia, as a result of a nasty ear infection.

Because they had already deemed me to be a Brooklyn wise-guy, my commanding officer placed me into a southern platoon full of fellow students from Georgia and South Carolina.

Unfortunately I received combat boots that were too small, and I was too proud to complain. During this time, I made a number of friends, and I volunteered for a 24-mile march carrying a Browning automatic rifle in 90-degree heat, wearing those boots that were too small for my feet.

I made it the distance, but as a result, I wound up with cellulitis, an infection of my cells, and I spent two months in the naval hospital in Quantico, VA. My legs were almost amputated.

I went into the reserves as a private as my legs were too damaged to go through this again. I always regretted not going back and becoming an officer, but I received an honorary discharge and became an honorary member of the Marine Corps. Coming back to 9-11, I was very proud that my son became a Major, went to war for his country, and he continues to make me proud daily. He is a doctor, an obstetrician, and is married to his wife, Karen, who is also a Major in the US Army, and who works today as a professor of medicine and oncology. They live in Florida with their three beautiful children.

Part of my therapeutic encounters was total praise for the veterans of this country, and those people who fought in this most difficult war. These are experiences that can never be emulated through books or through psychoanalytical training.

In order to reach some form of goal, one has to have an understanding of all these factors, and at the same time, the ability to empathize for all people going in harms' way.

All these factors from being out in the Brooklyn Streets, being a member of a gang, fighting people for no apparent reason outside of proving my machoism, gave me a deeper understanding of people who are going through difficult and challenging times, whether it be in the inner cities, in university settings, or on the forefront of war.

Much of my life was going through some very difficult, painful experiences, and at the same time, going through psychoanalytical and psych-therapeutic training, and learning the art of combining my own trauma with those of others, and researching phenomenon to validate many of my experiences.

It is also important to note that my first wife, Alan's mother, was a beautiful woman, an Israeli, who was a master sergeant in the Tank Corps in Israel. I suspect my son got some of his insight and military expertise from her.

Chapter 17

FATHERS' RIGHTS

Another major learning experience was my introduction to Fathers' Rights.

I suspect that my desire and involvement in the Fathers' Rights Movement and the National Parents' Rights Movement is that I have always tried to reunite with the father who abandoned me when I was a child.

For 20 years, I was the director of Fathers' Rights Metro and then the National Association for Fathers. That all began in 1983 when I moved back to New York and at the same time, found myself in a difficult custodial battle with Julia.

I went to a Fathers' Rights Metro meeting, and after mentioning what I had done in my life, I was elected president. I was responsible for helping that group grow from several hundred people to well over 2,000. One day, I accompanied my friend to Manhattan Supreme Court, and he asked me if I could testify for him in terms of his character – as a character witness.

I said sure, and so I went into Court for him, and without any knowledge of what the process was, was qualified as an expert in mental health. I helped this fellow get visitation of his children.

That was the first case. From there, my ability to testify as an expert spiraled out of control. I wound up testifying as an expert throughout the country, coast to coast, and in addition, have testified in Europe, Germany and Israel.

I believe that children are our link to eternity. For that reason, I became an advocate for both men and women to gain accessibility to their children. I made a great deal of enemies with matrimonial attorneys.

I have led demonstrations, and some of them got out of hand to the point where family court had to be closed because of the number of demonstrators who showed up. As a result, I was arrested for disturbing the peace, creating violent demonstrations, and court-officers being pushed and punched.

I acknowledged that I never had experience in leading demonstrations, and clearly it was not my specialty. Some of them definitely got out of hand.

I could never have predicted all the anger between litigants and the courts, many of whom were embroiled in lengthy custody battles. I was on national television. I was asked if I would be a guest on a television program, and I wound up on satellite television for two years on a program called Children of Divorce. As a result of this program falling in my lap, I had major celebrities throughout the country contacting me to testify on their behalf in their custody battles.

I was often accompanied by my associate, a brilliant, black leader, who was a former Black Panther, and we became good friends. His name is James Will. We were on television together and also on major national television such as CBS and NBC, and we both became co-founders of Fathers' Rights Metro. Children of Divorce aired on top of the Empire State Building, adjacent to the observation tower. I always had a fear of elevators, and I always waited for James to come to the base of the Empire State Building so we could climb the 102 floors together.

Chapter 18

KATHY: My Greatest Challenge

I have been married to Katherine Levine at the time of this writing for 23 years. She is a New York State Superior Court Judge, and is without a doubt the love of my life.

We have two beautiful children, Sophia and Moira. My daughters with Kathy came later in life for both of us, and they are one of our most cherished gifts.

My daughter Sophia attended Fiorella H. LaGuardia High School of Music and Art and Performing Arts, and then moved on to Emory University in Atlanta, Georgia. She is loving and caring. She spent the summer of her sophomore year at Emory with congress woman Yvette Clark, helping minorities immigrate to the United States. She also played a key role in administering the congresswoman's office.

She spent her junior year in college at the Hebrew University in Israel. She is a master violist, plays beautifully, and she is very dear to all of us. She is bright, beautiful, feisty, and fights for causes in which she believes such as animal rights.

My daughter Moira also attends LaGuardia and is a master violist as well as a champion tennis player. I am so very proud of her.

Because I am older with Sophia and Moira, I have learned a lot about what to do and what not to do as a parent, and I truly believe I feel younger today because of the energy I so gratefully absorb from these beautiful girls.

I am sure without any hesitation that my daughters are becoming amazing young women because of the example and inspiration their mother has consistently demonstrated for them.

Kathy was and continues to be my greatest challenge. We met while she was senior counsel for the United Federation of Teachers. I was referred by Carolyn A. Kubitschek, a prominent civil rights attorney, who stated to Kathy, "If you want an expert who's not afraid, call Monty."

I wound up being Kathy's expert on a case, and low and behold, the sparks started flying and we eventually got married. Kathy, even though she is outspoken and very loud in the Courtroom, is at her heart, a soft, kind, loving person who has put up with my craziness for nearly a quarter century.

I give a great deal of credit to Kathy who has spent numerous days helping me deal with the uncertainty of life and has helped me navigate through some very difficult times. She is bright, feisty, pretty and has an amazing understanding of humanity. She has helped me advance my career. Recently, I helped her with her career and played a key role in her campaign race to become a New York Supreme Court Justice. It is interesting to note that she had more votes than anyone else in New York State.

Kathy has spent a great majority of her life fighting for civil rights for all types of minorities and some very dysfunctional people. She has worked tirelessly to make the world a better place, and she continues to do so every day when she sits on the bench.

I also can't thank enough all my pets, my beloved pit bulls, my beautiful turtles, that have always been there and have always been so loyal.

It is important to note, that while I had difficult times in the various marriages, I had a burning desire to keep all of my children together. To this day we have a family reunion every year. Several years ago, my children organized a 75th birthday bash and roasted me in a New York nightclub. I have seven beautiful grandchildren.

On a side note, I mention that during my first and second custodial disputes, I had an extreme panic that I would lose my children and would not be allowed to be a father. This, I believe, was because I did not see my father for 16 years, and therefore, suffered from an anxiety disorder throughout a great deal of my life.

I understood that if I was ever going to help anyone therapeutically, I had to understand his/ her psychological history. I had to empathize with them and rather than judge them, understand how they got from point A to point B.

Chapter 19

CONNECTING THE DOTS:

One can never truly understand what goes on in other people's minds.

As I was working on this book with my administrator, Vickie Taylor, I experienced a tragedy which will take me years to overcome.

In the early fall of 2016, I was paying my respects to a dear attorney friend of mine. Her husband, to whom I was very close, was a prominent psychiatrist practicing in several hospitals in New York. My friend's daughter came home to find her father hanging, dead, suddenly and without warning.

We all went through a year of total shock.

My dear friend was trying to help out a fellow psychiatrist who was to freely giving out prescriptions for pain medications, and who had been arrested on numerous charges, mainly for prescribing painkillers to patients around the clock.

Because of the good nature of my dear friend, he offered to help out the other psychiatrist's patients to allow the patients to continue their care since their doctor had been arrested. However, after my friend momentarily took over the practice, he too was arrested. It was a drastic, devastating turn of events, and my friend could not deal with the blow to his reputation.

Before my friend's suicide, I had assisted in helping him secure a prominent attorney whom I knew through New York circles and who also had several major movie actor clients. He was in the process of preparing my friend's criminal defense.

However, shortly after my friend was released from jail and was waiting for his trial to commence, he committed suicide.

This selfish act placed a severe burden on his family. I shake my head. I am sad beyond belief. This was a tragedy, a senseless loss of life. No problem is so great that one cannot push through it, turn it around. I miss my friend.

I paid my respects, and the day after the funeral, I called up another close friend of mine who is also a prominent attorney in the New York area. I was faced with yet another crisis. My friend was grieving. His beloved 17-year-old son had committed suicide that morning by jumping off a New York bridge.

This was very difficult for me to process.

The son's mother and father had come to me with their child in search of psychotherapeutic intervention one month prior to this event.

I quickly realized it was best for me to refer the son to other therapists given my close relationship to his parents. I did not want to be in a dual relationship with the father, while also working as a family therapist. It would be very difficult for me to point out any short comings of my friend, and still maintain my relationship with him.

When the son committed suicide, I realized no matter what therapists know or learn along the way, one cannot go through any form of recovery without some supportive therapy.

The feelings are immense, especially when one is dealing with young adolescents who do not express their inner feelings or are unable to do so.

In my opinion, part of the problem that young adolescents have today is that we are living in a very technocratic world where people relate through computers and smart phones and social media, and the personal touch between therapist and their patients in this modern age is diminished.

Yet it is imperative during this time, probably more so than ever before, for people to have that personal contact.

We are constantly getting double messages, which I have written about ad nauseum while I was writing columns on terrorism for the American Psychotherapy Journal.

The double messages that we are getting is that on one hand the authorities tell us that we have to be extremely suspicious of our surroundings because we are living in a world where terrorists are running around, blowing up people and buildings.

On the other hand, if we get too suspicious, we are told that we are paranoid, and we should not be so suspicious.

The younger generations are constantly getting a double message: They are living in an extremely cautious, suspicious place, yet they are reaching out to have a relationship with their peers and total strangers through their modern technology, their computer "profiles," on Snap Chat, Instagram and Facebook.

I learned a great deal when I was writing these columns on terrorism, and published approximately 25, peer-reviewed journal articles for the American Psychotherapy Association.

I soon found myself following all major terrorist attacks. Every time an attack was reported, I did what I could to learn more about it. I tried to identify why certain people committed certain offenses.

I tried, to the best of my ability, to track down these various individuals with their pathology.

As a result of this, I found out that many of these people grew up in very lonely, desperate lives, and pathology is the same whether you are a Muslim, Christian or Jew.

The unfortunate thing is that we cannot comprehend some of the dynamics of what is happening without having a deeper understanding of what makes certain individuals do what they do.

I feel that my training was not only in books and in psychoanalysis, and taking numerous hours of seminars and post-graduate work at Harvard. Where I really learned was being out in the streets and dealing with true, life experiences and individuals in a hands-on approach.

One cannot be a therapist without being out on the streets, dealing first-hand in decisions which affect patients and other peoples' lives. One cannot be a therapist by only working in a vacuum and not being part of the process.

For me, my biggest life-altering experience and the one that attracted me to the National Association for Fathers (which I led for 10 years with thousands of members throughout the country), was that my father left me very early in life. I did not see him again until I was approximately 16 years old. His involvement and connection to various organized crime organizations allowed me to teeter-totter between being law-abiding and studious, while exploring the gun-toting, dangerous, criminal dynamic of my family ties.

I am so thankful that the therapist's chair was a much more comfortable fit for me.

I grew up tough – but I'm helping people.

Chapter 20

THE TORAH

In June 2017 I received a call from Tom Shallow. I had worked with him approximately seven or eight years earlier on a case and he became a very close friend of mine.

After spending much time with his family, making numerous home visits and being appointed to do an evaluation, I wound up testifying on his behalf and realizing that the judge who was handling the case did not want to give him any parenting time. I testified, was qualified as an expert, and discovered that we had an uphill battle before us to get Tom parenting time.

Tom had rotten luck with attorneys. He realized that at the end of the day, he would be better off if he simply defended himself. He then brought me on board to aid him in his courtroom endeavors. After several years of litigation, his case went through the US Federal Court of Appeals and finally, all the way to the US Supreme Court.

Tom was eventually awarded joint parenting time of his beloved children, and through the process, we became very close friends.

Tom at one point in his career became the head of Veteran Affairs in Philadelphia, Pennsylvania, and did a great deal of work advocating on behalf of Veterans of Foreign Wars.

One day out of the blue in June 2017, Tom called me. He told me that he taken possession of a Torah, an Old Testament that was believed to be approximately 300 years old. He told me the Torah had somehow ended up in the hands of the US Navy and had been stored in the Philadelphia Navy Yard. It was saved by the Navy and had been on display in a Navy chapel which commemorated a World War II destroyer ship that had been torpedoed during WWII. According to history books, several chaplains of all faiths (Jewish, Catholic and Protestants), gave their life jackets to the sailors, and the chaplains went down with the ship. My friend Tom was assisting in organizing a major commemoration event, and he wanted to present the Torah to me, and I would then give it to Rabbi Joseph Potasnik.

Rabbi Potasnik gained fame after the bombing of Sept. 11, 2001, as he was at the time one of the chaplains for the New York City Fire Department, and he opened the doors of his congregation to those fleeing the bombing of 9-11. I also learned that Rabbi Potasnik had lost family during WW II.

This event was attended by numerous civil servants in Philadelphia and New York City. My wife, New York Justice Katherine Levine was one of the speakers during the ceremony.

We had in attendance various Navy officials of all ranks, police officials, fire department officials, as well as Jewish, Catholic and Protestant Chaplains.

Also invited to the ceremony was one of the few surviving soldiers who was on General George S. Patton's Staff during World War II and was a member of the American Liberating Forces. They assisted in the liberation of the people in Dachau, one of the horrific Nazi Concentration Camps in southern Germany. Also in attendance was a survivor of Dachau. The speeches and experience of this ceremony were inspiring, humbling, and it was truly amazing to hold the Torah in my hands.

This Torah somehow survived World War II and was given by Catholic Chaplains to the Navy. It was a great honor to be a part of this all day event. We had a special ceremony in which Tom opened up the Jewish Museum to the group of attendees and then invited us to a special dinner commemorating the liberation of the concentration camps.

The Navy Yard in Philadelphia left me feeling like I was in a state of suspended animation as I drove through it looking out over the World War II Battleships, destroyers and submarines.

I held the 300-year-old Torah in my hands, and then I gave it to Rabbi Potasnik, who has since given it to the Congregation Mount Sinai, and it is utilized during their services.

Chapter 21

THERAPY IN 2017

This spring, I came back from a meeting with an attorney and my client. We had worked three hours on trying to reach an agreement so that our client could have some form of parenting time with his child. Father is a warm individual, but slightly naïve and not cognizant of all the loop-holes in the system.

He had picked me up that morning, and was returning me home in his bright yellow Camaro, what I can only describe as a replica of a bumblebee car for super heroes, when he ran out of gas on the Brooklyn Expressway – a fast-moving highway, known for high traffic and miserably fast speeds.

As I sat there, waiting for him to figure out how to get gas so we could get the car going again and get out of this very precarious situation, I became reflective of my life.

The natural thing, based on my personality, would be that because I am histrionic, one who is known for showing emotions, being very verbally expressive in both satisfactory and unsatisfactory conditions, I typically should have lost my cool.

Instead, I thought why would I get angry about this at this stage in my life?

I just sat there, while cars were passing us by at 75 mph, and I started laughing.

Thankfully, a very nice woman pulled over and helped us. She drove my client to get gas while I sat alone, in reflection, waiting in the car.

The only reason I'm saying this is because I have to remember to not get stuffy, not to take things too seriously. Breathe. Reflect. Keep perspective.

At the end of the day, basically, we are all human. No one is perfect. These things happen.

This brings me to another memorable experience: I accompanied a doctor in court who not only had a medical degree, but also had a graduate degree from Emory University, Georgia, and a master's degree in public health. His wife, a Filipino, was planning on taking their son out of the country, and probably, that would have been the end of him seeing his beautiful son. Chances were high that she wasn't coming back. Even the law guardian, who hated me for some unknown reason started maligning me.

I was able to turn around the case because I knew the law guardian had never gone to see the son, and therefore, had no first-hand knowledge about which she could testify.

What further tilted the case in our favor was that the Judge ordered the law guardian to speak to me.

To the law guardian, it was something she could not deal with for whatever reason. They capitulated and stipulated to reverse custody. At the end of the day, however, my client simply gave up and walked away from his son because he did not want to continue to fight.

Throughout the last three decades, I have had the opportunity to testify on behalf of many parents, fathers and mothers, all across the United States on the phenomenon of parental alienation. When we win, it means children are going to maintain a relationship with their estranged, alienated parent. I always believe that prevailing on a case is more about the children than the client. At the end of the day, children need both parents.

I think most of my insight in all of these cases comes from spending the majority of my young life being on the streets and learning to spar with some very difficult individuals. I also observed my father and his misdeeds of being totally intertwined with organized crime.

To my astonishment, I realized that our current President Donald Trump's mentor was an attorney named Roy Cohn, a monster in his profession. I remember him as the same person who dropped by my father, Bill Abel's house on numerous occasions for a light-night scotch. It is hard to believe that our paths crossed, but I was only a little boy, and I vividly remembered Cohn visiting my father and talking about who knows what.

Chapter 22

Parental Alienation – A Reflection on Severe Alienation Cases

I have been working as a family therapist and expert witness in the field of custodial disputes for half a century. In every custody case in which I have been involved, one party (the mother or father) always wins everything (financial and children) and the other person loses everything. There are still many couples who have remained married for years, have raised children and grandchildren, and who, despite their differences, fostered ongoing, loving relationship with their children.

Unfortunately, in the U.S., more than 50 percent of marriages end in divorce, and numerous contentious divorces remain unresolved for years.

I have noticed in many of these cases, a number of which will be mentioned, that once a court proceeding starts, and legal experts, mental health experts and other members of the "Divorce industry" get involved, things spiral out of control. The case becomes a war, feelings of hatred are incited and encouraged, and the case becomes difficult if not impossible to be resolved. Various mental health experts add to this conflict by adding fuel to the fire by co-counseling the case with one side, rather than attempting to resolve the adversarial relationships by recognizing every ones differences. I have also noticed that one parent always postures him or herself as the future custodial parent (the more "fit" parent) and systematically and methodically attempts to remove the other parent from the child or children's lives. Then at the end of the divorce rainbow, deservingly or not, he or she will obtain child support and be designated the "custodial parent" until the children are adults.

Today, a number of experts call the phenomenon of one parent systematically and methodically removing the other parent from the children's lives **parental alienation** and/

or **parental alienation syndrome**. Without making this more complex, the syndrome is a more severe form of alienating the child or children against the targeted parent. This syndrome comes in many forms, such as creating a feeling among vulnerable children that the other parent is the devil incarnate, and that everything the other parent does has no merit. In this syndrome, the alienating parent minimizes everything the other parent does. After a while, children, who are already vulnerable to their parents' divorce, influence and belief systems begin to internalize these suggestions and start creating fantasy stories that everything the other parent does has an ulterior motive. This is done to hurt and destroy the other parent, also known as the **targeted parent or victimized parent**.

Through the years I have testified and been qualified as an expert in the area of parental alienation, and because my field of study is family therapy, I have identified the parent that is the perpetrator of this phenomenon as the **Identified Patient or the alienator.** The following cases that I have worked on showed a common thread of alienation.

CASES:[1]

1) <u>New Jersey</u> - This case involved children, ages 11 and 14, who were living in Texas with their father, while their mother resided in New Jersey, which had been the children's home. The father, for years, went on a rampage and portrayed the mother as an egregious person who did not know what she was doing, and who did not have the children's best interests at heart. He also portrayed the mother as someone who was heartless and not nurturing. The mother, after hearing about my work, consulted with me in my Greenwich Village office. I also brought my associate Karen Wagner, a Harvard-trained educator, into the case. The father, instead of becoming more conciliatory, became more aggressive, and refused to allow the children to have any contact with their mother or her experts. The mother was a warm, nurturing individual who loved her children. Karen Wagner and I testified for the mother and we obtained full custody for the mother. That was in 2010. As of now, the children do not want to return to their father and the mother is the sole custodial parent. The Court eventually halted parenting time with the father because on the children's final visit to Texas, the father again did not want to return the children and attempted to again turn them against their mother.

---

1   Given the privileged nature of these cases I have omitted the names of the parties.

2) <u>Florida</u> - I testified years ago in Brevard County, Florida, where the father did not have any parenting time with his two children, ages 8 and 10. The mother made numerous allegations of abuse against the father and called child welfare services to complain that the father was an egregious character who should not have any parenting time. The mother kept alienating these children, telling them lies about their father and even going so far as to direct the children to run away from the Fathers' home during his parenting time. I testified as an expert in parental alienation, and custody was reversed. As of now, the father enjoys shared custody with the mother. When I revisited the case recently, the children appeared to be happy and well adjusted.

3) <u>North Carolina</u> - I testified in North Carolina for a father who had no parenting time with his children, ages 4 and 5, even though he was a warm individual and a successful tax attorney in a large city. I testified about what would happen in several years if the father was not allowed parenting time with the children and educated the court on the phenomenon of parental alienation. The court then granted the father liberal visitation. The mother then refused to comply with the court's order that the children live part time with the father and the court found the mother guilty of contempt and sentenced her to six months in the county jail. (I did not ask for that consequence.) As a result of the mother's conduct, the court awarded full custody to the father. As of now, to the best of my knowledge, the children are living in a tranquil, harmonious relationship with their father, and at the same time, are seeing their mother with liberal parenting time.

4) <u>Alabama</u> – In this prominent case on parental alienation, the father began a new family after his divorce from his first wife. The mother received full custody and has raised her son, who is now 14, by constantly aborting parenting time between the father and his son and continually denigrating the father, his new wife, and the boy's step and half siblings. This resulted in the son becoming very alienated from his father and developing hostility towards the father. The thesis of my testimony was that unless there was intervention by the son's therapist, there would be severe psychological damage to the child. This case is pending a Court's decision and the father has been attempting to see his son for almost ten years.

5) <u>Pennsylvania</u> – I testified for a prominent dentist whom the Judge had ordered to have only supervised parenting time with his children. The children were ages 11 and 13. The mother, who was also a prominent dentist (both parents

had strong ties to a major university), prevented the children from visiting the father and accused him of being selfish, mean and abusive, none of which were validated. The children were so alienated that they refused to see the father. I testified to parental alienation. The Judge did not reverse custody, but awarded the father liberal parenting time and lectured the mother to stop the alienation or custody would be reversed. My Associate, Karen Wagner, conducted reunification therapy with the father and the children.

6) California – I testified for a mother several years ago in Los Angeles. The father, who was a prominent producer, was constantly undermining the mother during his parenting time, post-divorce. Their child was 9 at the time. I testified to the egregious effects of parental alienation and what was likely to happen if mother did not get some parenting time. Mother won custody of the child in this matter, and as of now, the father has liberal parenting time. The Court recognized parental alienation.

7) New York – I also testified for a Father who did not have any parenting time with his children, ages 13 and 14, for a number of years. The mother portrayed the father as a horrific individual who should not have any parenting time with his children. She also denigrated the Fathers' religion - Jewish - and refused to raise the children in the Jewish faith, although the parents agreed to this at the children's time of birth. The children were so alienated that they would send hate e-mails to the father. I testified in this matter to reverse parenting time. The court recognized the necessity of family therapy and the phenomenon of parental alienation. Therapy began in this case to assist in repairing the damaged relationships.

8) Georgia – I testified for a prominent business man who was the father of a 15-year-old daughter. There were numerous motions filed with the Court that this father smoked marijuana and for that reason should have a limited relationship with his child. I testified a number of times that the father had a strong bond with the child. The Fathers' purported marijuana use was a catalyst the mother used to reduce Fathers' parenting time. Ironically, the mother had been adjudicated as an alcoholic but had still been given greater parenting time. I testified about parental alienation and the devastating effects if the child continued to lose time with the father. The Judge, in his wisdom, gave the father a shared parenting schedule. The father is no longer engaging in any substance abuse, and the child is flourishing in a joint-custody atmosphere.

9) <u>Wisconsin</u> – I testified in Wisconsin for a female attorney and was accompanied by Ms. Karen Wagner. The mother was accused of alienating her three children against the father, an executive of a major pharmaceutical company. I was deposed and then testified for several days. The Court recognized parental alienation. However, the opposing party accused my client of being the alienator as well as having a substance abuse problem. Ironically, the father had an affair with the nanny and forced the mother out of the house. Prior to my entering the case, the court had awarded temporary custody to the father. We attempted to establish, through my testimony, that the mother had not been alienating the children, which was impossible as the mother hardly ever saw the children. In the end, mother's role was restored with liberal parenting time, a step up from the previously-ordered supervised visitation.

Symptoms:

The major aspect of parental alienation is a campaign of denigration and hatred towards the other parent. Parental Alienation also involves one parent planting ideas about the other parent in the children's psyches that have no basis in reality, and the children's rationalization about these ideas. The children exhibit a lack of ambivalence toward the targeted (victim) parent. When one cognitively perceives another person, they have many images of that person. An alienator accentuates a negative image rather than noting anything positive about the parent who is being targeted. The children therefore lose the healthy ability to see all parts of the alienated parent. For example, in the Colorado case described above, the father is physically 6-feet, 3-inches, and weighs close to 280 pounds. Rather than portraying the father as warm, kind, fuzzy and nurturing, the mother portrayed him as an intimidating, dangerous monster. **The way a mother portrays a father, or vice-versa, has a residual effect on the children's impressions.**

Another part of alienation is that the children become accomplices in the alienation of the victim parent. The children give support and confirmation of the <u>programming parent</u> and identify with the alienator during the alienation process. Another factor is <u>reflexive support</u> of the programming parent where the children are alienated not only from the victim parent but from any member of that parent's friends and family. The children lose all guilt in treating the alienated parent in a horrible manner. The alienation usually includes grotesque scenarios and inquisitions by the children against the targeted parent.

Many mental health experts identify parental alienation and parental alienation syndrome (PAS) as being two separate parts of the alienating phenomenon with the syndrome being on the more severe end of the spectrum. I also believe, from my work in this area, that PAS is just a more severe form of the alienating process.

COURT ACCEPTANCE OF PARENTAL ALIENATION SYNDROME

Some authors, particularly in the feminist literature, have claimed that Parental Alienation Syndrome does not exist. These individuals are unable (or unwilling) to admit that mothers as well as fathers can and do use the children as weapons in a conflicted custody fight. They contend that it is merely an excuse for abusers to blame their victims.

As a result, parties and judges may wonder about the concept and what weight to give it. Clever attorneys sometimes exploit this uncertainty hoping to shield an alienating parent from consequences, claiming PAS may not meet the so-called "Daubert" or "Frye" legal standards.

My actual experience in hundreds of cases confirms that the phenomenon is real whatever it may be called, and that the criticism is vastly overblown.

Nearly all judges in my cases took a practical view despite conflicting claims about formal labeling in psychological benchmarks and the niceties of legal classification. Judges detest alienating conduct by parents, and by adjusting testimony to the state and the individual court where the case is being heard, alienating parents can be held accountable.

I have also found that judges appreciate parents that take the trouble to educate the court through an appropriate expert in thoughtful court presentation.

❖

Letters
Of
Thanks
&
Awards

OFFICE OF THE PRESIDENT

BOROUGH OF BROOKLYN
CITY OF NEW YORK

Citation

*W*hereas, it is a time-honored Brooklyn tradition to recognize those rare and extraordinary organizations and individuals whose steadfast commitment to public service greatly improves the quality of life of all Brooklynites; and

*W*hereas, District Leader, 44th Assembly District Jacob Gold and the New Independent Democrats have gathered for their Annual Awards Dinner to pay tribute to those who have demonstrated a steadfast commitment to the betterment of their neighborhoods and communities, and the great Borough of Brooklyn, and to recognize Dr. Monty Weinstein; and

*W*hereas, on behalf of all Brooklynites, I salute Dr. Monty Weinstein, Director of the Family Therapy Center, a clinical fellow of the American Association for Marriage and Family Therapy and a fellow of the American Ortho-Psychiatric Association, serving parents and children during the difficult time of divorce, in addition to his service as Chairman of the Board for the National Parents Rights Association, I commend him for his unwavering commitment to support, guide and help to heal families that have undergone the hardship and emotional trauma of divorce, I congratulate him as he is duly recognized here today, supported by his wife Civil Court Judge Katherine A. Levine and their children Moira and Sophia, Lemore, Jacqueline and Dr. Alan Weinstein, extended family and friends, and I thank him and all those present for helping to make Brooklyn a better place to live, work, and raise a family;

*N*ow, therefore, I, Marty Markowitz, President of the Borough of Brooklyn, do hereby confer this citation on

Dr. Monty Weinstein

*I*n witness whereof, I have hereunto set my hand and caused the seal of the Borough of Brooklyn to be affixed this 28th day of April 2010.

April 28, 2010

Dear Dr. Weinstein,

I wish I could be joining you and the New Independent Democrats this evening as you are recognized for your outstanding community leadership. It gives me great pleasure to send greetings and congratulations. It is a well deserved honor and I wish you and your wife, Judge Katherine Levine, a memorable and enjoyable evening.

Your tremendous contributions to the children of New York as well as Georgia have impacted so many families and exemplify the American tradition of citizen service. Your leadership as the Director of the Family Therapy Center for the past twenty years has done such remarkable work for those parents undergoing divorce who want access to their children. In the most difficult times of individual's lives, you and your organization are there to help families ease the pain and struggles of divorce. Your role as Chairman of the Board for the National Parents Rights Association is a crucial outlet for countless families to seek support in a time of incredible need.

The renowned recognition in the field of psychology you have received is well warranted. By serving as a fellow of the American Ortho-Psychiatric Association and by sitting on the Board of Directors of the National Psychological Association, you are able to author columns and journals to help analyze and end the suffering of children tormented by the effects of violence. You are an example of the spirit of citizen service that is so vital to our democracy and to the well-being of children and families throughout New York and our nation as a whole.

Thank you for your tremendous leadership and for giving so much of your talents to the children of our state. Please accept my congratulations on tonight's hono my best wishes for a wonderful celebration and evening.

Warm Regards,

Kirsten E. Gillibrand
United States Senator

www.kirstengillibrand.com ★ 15 West 26th Street, Suite 4R ★ New York, New York 10C
Telephone: (212) 481-2010 ★ Fax: (917) 591-7849

Paid for by Gillibrand for Senate

CHRISTIAN LAW CENTER

Suite 112
2701 East Chapman Avenue
Fullerton, CA 92831-3798

Mailing Address
Post Office Box 4189
Fullerton, CA 92834-4189

Telephone (714) 738-8822
Facsimile (714) 738-4439

Thursday, January 02, 2003

Myron "Monty" Weinstein, Ph.D.
Central Intake
Family Therapy Center for New York & Georgia, Inc.
1780 E. 26th St.
Brooklyn, NY 11229
Tel.& Fax (718) 382-1293
e-mail: DrMonty1@aol.com
Credentials – call (914) 794-7900
www.familyunity.com

FAX TRANSMITTAL
Time: 4:32 PM

Re: In re: a Post Dissolution of Marriage Child Custody Dispute re:
        Minor Child
        Superior Court of the State of California, County of San Bernardino,
        San Bernardino District Case No. SBFL 36681

Dear Dr. Weinstein:

I have been a practicing attorney for over 28 years.

Prior to entering the practice of law, I earned a Bachelor's Degree in Electrical Engineering from Loyola University of Los Angeles, worked on the Apollo Man on the Moon Program, and as Rocket Scientist. My background includes six (6) lifetime California Community College teaching credentials in the subject areas of Law, Real Estate, Engineering, Industrial Machine & Related Technologies, Mathematics and Philosophy & Religion. For over 20 years, I was also a licensed California Real Estate Broker. In earning my Juris Doctorate degree, I was invited to and did participate as an author in the prestigious law review. In 1972, I was admitted to the United States Patent Bar. My further credentials include an Honorary Doctor of Divinity degree and both my wife and I are ordained Christian ministers.

For more than 16 years of my 28 years engaged in the practice of law, about eighty (80%) of my cases involved Family Law Matters under the banner of Christian Law Center.
During the year 2002, you were engaged by   to testify in this post-dissolution of marriage change of child custody case.

A number of major, cutting edge issues involving child custody modification are involved in this case. This case represents a mother's attempt to protect her son from a life-time of irreversible psychological

Myron "Monty" Weinstein, Ph.D.   *FAX TRANSMITTAL*
Central Intake   Time: 4:33 PM
Family Therapy Center for New York & Georgia, Inc.

Re:

Monday, September 09, 2002
Page 2 of 2

damage. She has but a single goal - to protect her son from the continuing mental and sex abuse permitted by his father.

Your in-depth, lengthy experience and university credentials in this highly complex and specialized area of the law are most impressive.

Your testimony was not only extremely helpful in this case, but was cost effective as well.

One of the most significant benefits that you personally brought to this most difficult battle is your immediate and continuing compassionate interest in Ms. Bruno's horrific case which goes far beyond your fees.

The two words that aptly describe your activities in this case would be "competent caring."

I look forward to working with you again in the future and would hardily recommend your services to others seeking an extraordinary expert in their family law matters.

Always my best to you, Dr. Weinstein.

Very truly yours,

Ben E. Lofstedt
Attorney at Law

BEL/dms

Thomas J. Shallow

Pennsylvania

March 14, 2008

To Whom It May Concern:

I write this letter of recommendation in support of Dr. Monty N. Weinstein.

My name is Thomas J. Shallow and I have two children, a daughter, now aged 13, and a son, now age 15. When I first met Dr. Weinstein my children were ages five and seven, I had been stripped of my parental legal custody, removed from my own home, and relegated to a mere biweekly visitor in the life of my son and daughter.

A year earlier I had entered the family court system in the county where I live in an attempt to put an end to the abuse that my children and I were regularly being subjected to at the hands of the children's mother. My now, ex wife would fly into uncontrolled outbreaks of violence and obscene behavior. Screaming and yelling was regularly punctuated with slapping punching and pulling the children's hair. Outbreaks would regularly continue for 15 to 45 minutes followed by a recalcitrant personality who would offer apologies for the damages incurred or the physical violence inflicted in her uncontrolled moments. I would come home from work to discover my children being abused by their uncontrolled mother who handled them like rag dolls. This was a woman that in order to avoid her pummeling, I would have to barricade myself in a room and while there, as I held the door shut, she would stand in the hall and screen "you're hurting me", "you're hurting me"???. Never once did I ever raise a hand to her nor did she ever report that in the over 3600 pages of testimony that entered the record in our case. Yet, in her fits of anger she drew blood on both the children and I.

Just before my custody case went to trial my wife began seeing a psychiatrist who put her on a regimen of psychotropic medication twice daily and directed her to see a therapist weekly. At trial my wife reported that she was "a new woman". The results of Mother's psychological testing were craftily glossed over and largely covered up. The court ordered psychologist that was imposed in our case had an established track record of mortgaging the family's future so that mother might be rehabilitated. I was not prepared to deal with a sexually biased family court system that was so willing to sacrifice my children to support their desire to be politically correct. I later came to understand that in family court, men and their love for their children are nothing less than meat, relegated to the importance of a paycheck, and the court system is simply a meat grinder. The court excused its decision to rehabilitate mother by falsely characterizing me as having been insensitive and unsupportive of mother, a conclusion not remotely supported by the record. In much the same way as an unscrupulous law enforcement official might place a gun in the hands of an innocent individual improperly shot; the family court system covers its tracks. There is no jury of 12 in the family court, there is only a judge who, in the absence of expert testimony, can easily fabricate an opinion and decision not rooted in truth but crafted so as to give an appearance of proper judicial conduct.

When Dr Weinstein entered my case he exposed the test results, and the finding of mother's mental illness that the original Court ordered psychologist had covered up. Dr. Monty Weinstein is a truly extraordinary individual who genuinely loves children. In his extensive experience he has seen the impact of divorce and separation on the pawns of Family Court, the children. Biased, cronyism, and in chamber deals, seldom consider the indelible scars that a child of divorce is forced to endure. Dr. Weinstein clearly understands a child's pain and need to have access to the love and nurturing of both parents. In his years of experience he has seen and can predict what happens to a child who grows into a man or a woman and is a victim of an ignorant court system. Dr. Weinstein is an expert in many areas of the mental health profession but he is first last and always a child advocate.

No court system wants to be exposed for its inadequacies and least of all exposed for their arrogance, biased, or misinformed decisions. The family court judge has vast power over the American family and the litigants who dare to enter their realm. There are few professionals who are willing to take on a county-based family court system that regularly demonstrates little respect for the rights of a parent. Dr. Weinstein is one extraordinary individual who, if he believes in your case, will walk into the fires of hell to throw water on the black robes of Satan so a child can have appropriate access to their parents.

My personal journey through the court system has navigated the County Family Court, the state, Commonwealth of Pennsylvania and the Federal Courts of the United States. Mine is a story of a Father who not unlike millions of Fathers across our country genuinely loves his children and wants more than anything to actively be in their lives as they grow. The mental health establishment universally recognizes the importance of Fathers in the lives of children, but, by contrast, the Family Court Systems in America do not endorse or support the importance of Fathers' role in the family. It was Dr. Weinstein who made it possible for me to have access to my children. With Dr. Weinstein's assistance the court returned to me shared legal custody of my children and 35% of physical custody.

Today, and for the past 2 years, I have had 100% of the physical custody of my 15-year-old son. My 13-year-old daughter however has been largely alienated from both her brother and myself. As of five months ago she began living exclusively with her mother. Years ago, three experts predicted that my daughter's relationship with both my son and I would become the victim of alienation. That information was supplied to the court. The original judge in the case followed by the second judge in our court case ignored the best interest of the children by suppressing the evidence and deliberately implementing stall tactics that were aimed at my further financial devastation. The children in family court are regularly the last to be considered. In my quest for justice I took the second judge involved in my case along with the County and three other co-defendants through the federal court system and ultimately to the steps of the Supreme Court of the United States.

Four different attorneys including the Chief Counsel for the Supreme Court of Pennsylvania argued in the Eastern District of Pennsylvania Federal Court that my case should be dismissed primarily on the merits that a federal court has no right to question the decisions of a state based court (Rooker -- Feldman Doctrine). Secondarily, the same attorneys argued that the Judge in my case, Thomas P. Rodgers, who was sworn to uphold the Constitution of the United States and had clearly failed to do so, when, he knowingly, willingly, and blatantly, violated the civil rights law, should, along with his codefendants get off under the protections of judicial immunity.

On further appeal the Third Circuit Court of Appeals overturned the Eastern District of Pennsylvania Federal Courts' earlier decision and ruled in my favor by denying opposing counsel's arguments for dismissal based on The Rooker – Feldman Doctrine. However, the Third Circuit Court upheld that the judge and the associated codefendants could hide behind the notion of judicial immunity. On February 25, 2007 a Petition for a Writ of Certiorari was filed in The United States Supreme Court to address the remaining question of whether a judge should disgracefully be allowed to hide his clearly improper conduct behind the protections of judicial immunity.

Only one in 800 cases that are filed in the Supreme Court of the United States are ever heard. A citizen has a better chance of being struck by lightning, one in 600, during his lifetime. On May 14, 2007 the Supreme Court of the United States entered an order denying my plea to hear the question raised in my Petition for a Writ of Certiorari.

My journey through the court system was largely the exception. Due to finances, I traveled a good portion of the road without a lawyer and represented myself Pro se. I did not have to turn away from what I believe to be my obligations as a Father, because I was fortunate enough to have the support of exceptional individuals like Dr. Weinstein.

Nowhere in the federal court system that led to the Supreme Court of the United States Petitioned did anyone say that the local county judge acted properly and did not violate federal law. In the end the federal court system upheld that the judge and his associates were immune. The Supreme Court of the United States denied my appeal to hear the case.

Throughout this arduous quest for my children's custody Dr. Weinstein and his expert team stuck with me in some of the darkest moments of my life. Without Dr. Weinstein's extraordinary insight and extensive resources I would not have been successful in having any role in the bringing up of my children. My only regret where Dr. Weinstein is concern is that I was not fortunate enough to have found him sooner. The major blunders in my case took place before Dr. Weinstein and I came in contact. I feel certain that if Dr. Weinstein could have been involved in the early stages of my litigation he would certainly have saved me and my children the years of pain and financial devastation that I now pray are behind me.

Without Dr. Weinstein's expert insight I would very likely have been just another father who desperately wanted to be in the lives of his children but was relegated to nothing more than a visitor. I probably would have ended up on a steam grate, broken by a court system who is remarkably without conscience.

Sincerely,
E-signed, sent via
Email
Thomas J. Shallow

10-21-13

Dr. Monty Weinstein,

My family thanks you for the time and dedication to the cause of getting Weld County in Colorado to understand our struggles. I have been suffering for the past 7 years desperately trying to get the court to recognize the alienation that was devastating my relationship with my children, me, and family.

In April of 2012 at the culmination of my worst fears, my oldest son gave in to the pressure of the alienation and refused to see me any further perpetrated by my ex-wife. As weeks turned into months of not seeing my oldest son, the younger two children began to follow suite from the venomous alienation.

Motions began to be filed by their mother to stop my parenting time. Filing a contempt that was denied, I became desperate knowing the court hasn't and wouldn't see things for what they were for I have tried in the past. As so many times before, I began to search on the internet for someone who would have the expertise needed to help me with what has seemed to be a never ending battle to maintain a relationship with my three children. It was only God that could have led me to such a seasoned individual in the matters that had plagued us from past until present.

I came upon your name Dr. Monty Weinstein on Google. I began to read your website and realized that no man had the vast knowledge you have acquired through the long road of re-unification of children to mothers and fathers over 50 years. No one could know better if my children were truly alienated better that you.

I actually prayed before I sent the email to you Dr. Monty thinking, "This guy won't have the time for me, if he does respond it will probably be a secretary a month to late and I will be seeing my children in supervised visitation". I received a call from you directly within hours of my email.

When you entered my case in May of 2012 my oldest son was refusing to see me and the younger two were in the process of doing the same. You were literally there for 72 hours and witness to the alienating behavior of my ex-wife and how it was affecting my children. 24 hours after you left and the filing of your first report I had my son back who I hadn't seen in 3 months and we were off on a much needed vacation thanks you Dr. Monty.

 Dr. Monty has come to visit my family many times. Through his excellent reports that cut to the chase, and his unsurpassable ability to testify against all odds/scrutiny along with the rut that the local court was in; you have truly improved my situation empowering me to continue in the relationship with my children. There has been a 180 degree turn in the courts view of my ex-wife who is a Doctor of Veterinary Medicine. For the first time the court has a grasp on who this women truly is and what her goal has been in the destruction of my relationship with my kids. Thanks to you Dr. Monty I have been able to start to normalize a relationship with my children and an enormous pressure has been relieved from my children, me, and family.

The most amazing thing I have found about you Dr. Monty is your love and commitment toward the re-unification of children and their parents. There aren't enough words that can be said for someone who will sacrifice so much of himself including his own time with his family to help others in need.

 Dr. Monty these are some of the words that describe you that led to the end result of my case for now: Determined, experienced, knowledgeable, affective, persistent, unmovable, faithful, professional, connected and most of all unequivocal. These are qualities that you brought forth in my case and so many others. It is my hopes that other professionals will step up to your level in this country and world and do great things as you have for you set the bar.

Your friend and most Sincerely,

Derek Stegner

10-21-13

LAW OFFICES OF
David Edward Oles

Tel: 770-753-9995 (Atlanta)   3526 Old Milton Parkway   davidsr@deoleslaw.com
Fax: 877-207-3883   Alpharetta, GA 30005   www.davidcoles.com

September 23, 2013

Dr. Monty N. Weinstein
1780 E. 26th Street
Brooklyn, New York 11229

      Re: *A v. S*
             Colorado District Court

Dear Dr. Monty N. Weinstein:

Please let me take this opportunity to express my sincere thanks on my own behalf, and on behalf of my client, for your able assistance in Colorado District Court. As you know, Dad was facing an attempt (one of many) to limit his parenting time with his children. The efforts brought and instigated by his former wife included multiple police reports claiming violence, multiple accusations to Colorado Child Services claiming abuse of the children, and multiple claims in family court seeking to limit or terminate Dad's relationship with the kids.

By everything I could see Dad is a fine father and his children love him dearly. However, they were alienated over a period of years, to where it became difficult for him to attend events, to enjoy weekends and vacation with them, and he had been banned from the kids' school. His oldest son was being torn in two, and experiencing severe anxiety and emotional anguish. A target of these repeated attacks, Dad was uncertain where to turn to get the help he needed.

You went "above and beyond" the requirements of this engagement. Thanks to your persistent, diligent, and patient efforts, we were able to carefully document and expose a pattern of alienation that had gone on for years. That we did so is clear from the result. The judge's language in the final order is unambiguous:

"Petitioner's behavior and apparent attempt to terminate the children's relationship with the Respondent gives this Court great concern. Petitioner has engaged in behavior that has a pervasive effect on the children's ability to freely express their love and affection for their father."

You were also instrumental in revealing a chronic and malicious effort by the children's "therapist" (a former domestic violence advocate) that reinforced false notions of an abusive father. Finding that she "has been used by Petitioner as a means to continue alienating the children from Respondent." The judge further concluded that she missed obvious signs that Mom had been coaching the children, and prohibited all further contact with the children, as "it is clear that allowing [her] to continue to be used as an instrument of alienation by Petitioner is inappropriate."

This case was particularly difficult given that to most other aspects, mother appeared to be a model parent, whose children were well-behaved, and accomplished in their education and achievements. It was only your patient observation and investigation that allowed the knot to be unraveled. Your dedication to this matter was evident, and even the court-appointed investigator testified that he had never seen an expert spend so much time on a case as you did on this one.

Without your vast experience, timely suggestions, persistent effort and masterful guidance I am convinced that we could not have achieved this dramatic and successful conclusion for our client.

Sincerely,

David Edward Oles, Esq.
GA Bar. # 551544

EPSTEIN BECKER & GREEN, P.C.
ATTORNEYS AT LAW
RESURGENS PLAZA
945 EAST PACES FERRY ROAD, SUITE 2700
ATLANTA, GEORGIA 30326

(404) 923-9000 PHONE
(404) 923-9099 FAX
www.ebglaw.com

DIRECT:
(404) 923-9078
kelwell@ebglaw.com

250 PARK AVENUE
NEW YORK, NEW YORK 10177-1211
(212) 351-4500

1227 25TH STREET, N.W.
WASHINGTON, D.C. 20037-1156
(202) 861-0900

1875 CENTURY PARK EAST
LOS ANGELES, CALIFORNIA 90067-2501
(310) 556-8861

ONE LANDMARK SQUARE
STAMFORD, CONNECTICUT 06901-2601
(203) 348-3737

TWO GATEWAY CENTER
12TH FLOOR
NEWARK, NEW JERSEY 07102-5401
(973) 642-1900

75 STATE STREET
BOSTON, MASSACHUSETTS 02109-1807
(617) 342-4000

TWO EMBARCADERO CENTER
SAN FRANCISCO, CALIFORNIA 94111-3994
(415) 398-3500

12750 MERIT DRIVE
DALLAS, TEXAS 75251-1248
(972) 628-2450

55 EAST MONROE STREET
CHICAGO, ILLINOIS 60603-5709
(312) 845-1999

October 29, 2002

Monty N. Weinstein, ~~M.D.~~ Psyd.
1780 East 26th Street
Brooklyn, New York 11229

      RE: Brown v. Greenspan
             Superior Court of Fulton County
             State of Georgia
             Civil Action File No.: 2002CV47602

Dear Dr. Weinstein:

    I would like to thank you for your testimony and other assistance in the above-referenced action. As you know, this case concerned difficult issues of visitation and child custody. Your testimony was instrumental in influencing the Court to strongly recommend co-parenting classes for Mr. Greenspan, overnight visitation, and graduated visitation as Matthew Greenspan matures. As you know, all of these issues were extremely important to our client, and you were no small part of our obtaining a good result for him.

    Enclosed please find several of my business cards your reference and use. Please feel free to contact me if you have any questions on this or any other matter. Again, it was a pleasure working with you, and I hope to have the opportunity to so again in the future.

             Sincerely yours,

             Kevin M. Elwell

KME:cdb
Enclosures

cc: Marc E. Rovner, Esq.
     Mr. Steven Greenspan

AT 97572 1

August 11, 2009

Dr. Monty N. Weinstein, Director
Family Therapy Center For New York and Georgia, Inc.
National Parents Rights
1780 East 26th Street
Brooklyn, NY 11229

Dear Dr. Weinstein:

Thank you for all the help and assistance you provided during my horrific custody trial. Your passion, vast experience as a forensic psychologist and expert witness, as well as your broad experience of over 2,500 cases you have represented were key to the success of being able to get my children returned to me from *another state* after nearly a year of separation from me.

You were very well prepared, your credentials were impressive to the court, and you were extremely credible on the witness stand. During cross examination there was no hesitation in your testimony – it was crisp, to the point, and made clear to the court your expert opinion and the impact the events were having on my children.

Furthermore, you worked as an integral part of the team representing my children and provided insights from your vast court experience, moral support, and were highly responsive throughout the entire process.

Words cannot describe how incredibly thankful and grateful I am for what you did for me and my children.

As you know, I have two children with my ex-husband. My daughter is almost 15, and my son is 13. During the divorce proceedings, my ex-husband relocated to Houston, Texas for some unknown reason. Our divorce was finalized in July 2005, and I was granted primary physical custody of our children and we reside in New Jersey.

In March 2006, my ex-husband filed an application with the court to transfer physical custody of our children to Houston, Texas. With the family court system being so overburdened, our hearing was continuously delayed. Weeks turned into months which became years.

During the summer of 2007, I sent both of our children to Houston, Texas to spend time with their father. Instead of returning our children to me at the end of the summer, as we had agreed and was court ordered, my ex-husband decided to register them for school and refused to return them to me at the end of the summer. Not only did my ex-husband refuse to return our children to me, he alienated them against me during their summer stay. They wanted nothing to do with me, and for the most part, they refused to even speak with me.

I was forced to file a petition with the New Jersey courts to compel my ex-husband to return our children to me from Texas. Due to the fact that our custody hearing was still an open case in the court system and that our children had already started school, the judge decided to allow our children to stay in Houston Texas until the completion of the trial. Not only was I completely devastated by the judge's decision, I felt utterly betrayed by the entire legal system as we already had a court order that clearly defined custody. Of course, the court's decision gave my ex-husband more fuel for his fire by allowing him to continue to illegally keep our children and also by allowing him to continue the parental alienation tactics that had already successfully been employed. My ex-husband knew the longer he kept our children in Texas the more difficult it would be for me to get them returned to New Jersey.

As soon as I received that devastating decision by the court, I knew that my children were in jeopardy and the legal battle ahead would be a perilous one. I also realized just how devious and evil my ex-husband could be and how he would go to any length, including breaking the law, to keep our children from me. At that point, I realized that in order to have our children returned to me and stop the damaging effects of parental alienation, I would to have to hire the best parental alienation/child custody expert I could find that was well seasoned in highly adversarial court settings and was a forensic psychologist without compare. Then I found you.

I started to research the internet and the name that kept coming to the top of each and every search was yours. I went to your website, and I realized I found exactly who I was looking for. I immediately sent you an email explaining my situation. I was hoping to get a response from you within a week or two, so I was astounded when you responded to me within a couple of hours!! You were out of town, traveling for another case, yet you found the time to respond to me and quickly started developing a plan of action. I knew I had found the right person to help me. I wanted someone who was not only knowledgeable and experienced; I wanted someone who was passionate about my children, had empathy for what I was facing, and would be willing to fight to the end.

We discussed how difficult my case was and how diabolical and vindictive my ex-husband was, yet you were still willing to take on my case. You took on my case with the full knowledge that it would be a vicious, all out war, and you never once wavered in your dedication and hard work to protect my children and help restore my custody. You were unbelievably responsive to every phone call, email, or court document whether it was from me or my attorney. You always made me feel as if my case was the only case you were working on
Not only did you bring your knowledge, experience, and passion to my case, you brought a world class team who is just as knowledgeable, qualified, and passionate in their areas of expertise. As far as I'm concerned, Karen Wagner and Suzanne Silver are not only an integral part of your team; they are amazing and wonderful people.

All in all, my entire custody case took over 3 ½ years to complete. Although our children have been back in my custody since June 2008 and the case finally came to an end in January 2009, I didn't received the court's decision until July 2009 which denied a transfer of custody of our children to my ex-husband and also sanctioned him for his bad behavior.

I would be happy to speak to any of your potential clients as a reference for you. You and your team worked under the most challenging circumstances yet you were tireless in your quest and dedication to protect my children and return them to me.

As I am witness to how you were able to get my children returned to me, I truly believe you'll be able to get anybody's children returned to them.

Once again, thank you.

Sincerely,

 E-signature

Constance A. Banfield

Iandoli, Edens & Weinberger, LLC

Chester Commons, 310 Route 24, Suite A4, Chester, NJ 07930

Josephine B. Iandoli, Esq. +
Ann M. Edens, Esq. +
Bari Z. Weinberger, Esq. *
Rebecca K. Li, Esq.
Michelle L. Olenick, Esq.
Amy Kriegsman, Esq. **
Stefanie C. Gagliardi, Esq.

Tel: (908) 879-9499
Fax: (908) 879-4841
Web: www.iewlaw.com

+ Accredited Divorce Mediators
* Certified by the NJ Supreme Court
as a Matrimonial Law Attorney
**Also admitted in the State of New York

August 13, 2008

Dr. Monty Weinstein
1780 East 26th Street
Brooklyn, N.Y. 11229

    RE: Banfield v. Banfield

Dear Dr. Weinstein:

    Your assistance in this case is most appreciated. It was wonderful to have someone known for his advocacy of father's rights, to be an expert for a mother who was alienated from her children. Not only do we appreciate your willingness to get involved in this case, but your willingness to jump right in and do whatever it took at any given time. When we needed reports on short notice, you were able to prepare reports on such short notice. When we needed testimony, you made yourself available for testimony. You were more than willing to give input into strategy so that we would have a cohesive presentation. Your involvement of other experts extremely experienced in their sub-specialties, we believe is not only helpful with respect to the outcome of the hearing, but will prove to be helpful to the individuals in this family.

    Your testimony was excellent and we were able to just sit back during the cross-examination. Quite obviously, no points were scored by the other side during the cross-examination. You did not let the cross-examiner get the better of you, and you certainly did not give the other side any material to use against our case. To the contrary, you were able to further drive home some key points during the cross-examination.

    Your assistance in this matter is most appreciated, and we certainly intend to request your assistance and expertise in our cases in the future.

                         Very truly yours,

                         Josephine B. Iandoli

                         Josephine B. Iandoli

JBI:tcm

January 22, 2008

Dr. Monty Weinstein
The Family Therapy Center
1780 East 26th St.
Brooklyn, NY 11229

Dear Dr. Monty:

This letter is to serve as a personal Thank You and Testimonial for everything that you have done for my beloved daughter Bailey and myself. In my line of work, I have had the pleasure and honor to meet some of the most successful and dynamic leaders of Corporations, Sport Franchises and Government. During these experiences I have met some First Class and Elite Class leaders in their respective entities. Without hesitation, I can say with certainty that Dr. Weinstein is not in the category of First Class or Elite Class, but rather, he is in a class by himself which is World Class. I have never met anyone with such a high level of expertise in their respective field. This is what makes Dr. Weinstein the number one authority in the arena of Child Psychology and Development and Parental Custody issues in the Nation.

I was truly blessed to find Dr. Weinstein when my custody case began in February of 2006. When I met Dr. Weinstein I had already had an Emergency Hearing and my local attorney had cut a backdoor deal with my ex-wife's attorney with a Temporary Consent Order. I thought that it was what it state, Temporary. I knew that something was not right with the way everything unfolded on my case. I knew my local attorney was way over his head and that there was a very good chance that I would lose my beloved daughter that I had raised after her mother abandoned the two of us when my baby was only 20 months old.

Dr. Weinstein flew into Atlanta and met with myself and my local attorney. It still amazes me to this day that after ten minutes of conversing with my attorney and reviewing all of the Court documents that Dr. Weinstein accurately assessed and called my case in ten minutes! To this day, everything was 100% right on target. A university cannot teach this, only 50 years of experience in your field can bring forth this bit of expertise.

For Dr. Weinstein to successfully operate on a case, he needs complete control of the case. Because most local attorneys are Type A personalities, it is a challenge to see an attorney give up control. It was obvious that my local attorney wanted nothing to do with Dr. Weinstein because he knew Dr. Weinstein had uncovered many fraudulent, abusive and unethical proceedings that were taking place in the Forsyth County Court System. It was a good old boy network. Dr. Weinstein uncovered that the opposing attorney had perpetrated a fraud upon the Court, with the aid of a Psychologist that fashioned an Affidavit supporting the fact that I should see my child on a very limited basis. The problem was, Dr. Weinstein uncovered that the Psychologist had violated the Psychological Code of Ethics on three counts. Dr. Weinstein also discovered that the opposing attorney had withheld evidence on the case as well. He urged me to retain an attorney which he could work with. That was done.

The Forsyth County Court System has the mentality of a "Mississippi Burning" county. The Chief Superior Court Judge Jeffrey Bagley was the Judge on my case. It was obvious that he did not like a couple of "top guns" what the Judge and opposing attorney referred to as "hired guns" coming into their redneck county. The County was determined to do things their own way. The problem was, the County Judicial System was out of their league. They were dealing with a WORLD CLASS expert in Dr. Weinstein. The result: **DR. WEINSTEIN'S EXPERTISE HAD THE WHOLE COUNTY RECUSED FROM MY CASE! NO JUDGE IN THE COUNTY WAS ALLOWED TO HEAR MY CASE AND IT WAS BEING RE-ASSIGNED TO A SENIOR STATE JUDGE, HUGH STONE. THIS WAS THE FIRST OF TWO UNPRECEDENTED RULINGS FOR THE STATE OF GEORGIA.**

Once Dr. Weinstein had the whole County recused on my case, things began to move quickly. The Second unprecedented ruling that occurred in my case happened in a Hearing before the Senior State Judge Hugh Stone. **IN A SEPTEMBER 4, 2007 HEARING IN THE STATE OF GEORGIA, SENIOR STATE JUDGE RULED DR. MONTY WEINSTEIN AS IMMINENTLY QUALIFIED IN THE STATE OF GEORGIA AND HE COULD SIT IN THE DEPOSITIONS AND ACTUALLY RUN THE DEPOSITIONS! THIS IS UNHEARD OF. THE OPPOSING COUNSEL OBJECTED SAYING THAT DR. MONTY WAS COACHING MY ATTORNEY AND MYSELF AND JUDGE STONE STATED: "COUNSEL MAYBE YOU DID NOT HEAR ME, DR. WEINSTEIN IS IMMINENTLY QUALIFIED AND HE CAN SIT IN THE DEPOSITIONS, RUN THE DEPOSITIONS AND COACH ALL HE WANTS."**

Needless to say, the complexion of my case changed after that. I went from losing my child to having her 50% of the time! My daughter and I were truly blessed.

Without hesitation, I can say that without Dr. Weinstein, I would have lost my child, she would be living in another state and I might have been able to see her once a month for a weekend.

Dr. Weinstein, this is a personal thank you from the bottom of my daughter and my heart. We are indebted to you forever and will be personal friends forever. Thank you for saving my daughter and working with a passion like I have never seen in a professional. The passion and expertise that Dr. Monty exudes in unlike any I have ever witnessed.

Dr. Monty, my daughter and I thank you for everything that you have done and you have now become part of our family. God Bless you and your family.

With Warmest Regards,

John W. Evans III

TRANSCRIPTS

PAULDING COUNTY

GEORGIA

2016

IN THE SUPERIOR COURT OF PAULDING COUNTY
STATE OF GEORGIA

```
_ _ _ _ _ _ _ _ _ _ _ _ _ _ _ )
                              )
                              )
███████████████████          )
                              )
          Plaintiff,          )
                              )
vs.                           )        CASE NO.  16-CV-████
                              )
███████████████              )
                              )
          Defendant.          )
                              )
_ _ _ _ _ _ _ _ _ _ _ _ _ _ _ )
```

TESTIMONY OF DR. MONTY WEINSTEIN

Before the Honorable Dean C. Bucci

Judge of the Superior Court

In the Paulding County Judicial Circuit

280 Constitution Boulevard, Dallas, Georgia 30132

On November 4, 2016

<u>APPEARANCES</u>

For the Plaintiff: Pro Se

For the Defendant:

███████████████████
Official Court Reporter
280 Constitution Boulevard
Dallas, Georgia 30132

Page 69

```
 1                    P R O C E E D I N G S

 2          (In open court in the Paulding County

 3     Courthouse, November 4, 2016.)

 4                         - - -

 5          THE COURT:  Ms. ████ you're the petitioner.  Do you

 6     want to call a witness?

 7          MS. ████  Yes, sir.  I call Dr. Monty Weinstein on

 8     the stand, and I would like to get him -- well, have him as

 9     an expert.  I have some documents over here.

10          THE COURT:  Sir, the witness stand is over here.

11          DR. WEINSTEIN:  I'm sorry.

12          THE COURT:  That's all right.

13                         - - -

14          (Whereupon, the witness approached the witness stand

15     and was duly sworn by the Court.)

16                         - - -

17          THE COURT:  So what I'll do is, I'll swear you in if

18     you'll raise your right hand.

19          DR. WEINSTEIN:  (Complied.)

20          THE COURT:  Do you swear or affirm that the testimony

21     you're about to give will be the truth and nothing but the

22     truth so help you God?

23          DR. WEINSTEIN:  Yes, I do.

24          THE COURT:  All right.  Please have a seat.

25          Sir, state your name please.

                                                              4
```

```
 1          DR. WEINSTEIN:  It's Dr. Monty Weinstein.

 2          THE COURT:  Weinstein.  Okay.  Thank you, sir.

 3          DR. WEINSTEIN:  You're welcome.

 4          MS. ███████  Okay.  Mr. Weinstein -- Dr. Weinstein has

 5     already been qualified by Judge Vinson.  So can we just --

 6          MS. █████████      Your Honor, I'd object.  If we're

 7     offering Dr. Weinstein as an expert, I would like the

 8     opportunity to voir dire him.

 9          THE COURT:  All right.  Well, what happened in a

10     temporary hearing doesn't bind the court here, so any

11     findings or evidence that was presented there, the rules

12     are different at a temporary hearing, so you'll have to --

13     you'll have to make out your case, and if you want to

14     tender him as an expert, then you'll have to lay that

15     foundation.

16          MS. ████████   Okay.  Okay.

17                       - - -

18  Whereupon,

19                    DR. MONTY WEINSTEIN

20  was called as a witness herein, and having first been duly

21  sworn, was examined and testified as follows:

22                    DIRECT EXAMINATION

23  BY MS. █████████

24     Q    So Dr. Monty, would you please tell the Court how you

25  -- what you do, your qualifications.
```
                                                              5

         A   Yes, I will as quickly as I can mention my education

2 and training and background.

3   I have a B.A. in philosophy and psychology from Ithaca

4 College.

5   I have a Master's in counselling psychology from St. John's

6 University. I then went back and took another 30 credits in

7 clinical psych from St. John's University.

8   I -- in addition to that, I have another Master's from New

9 York University graduate school -- at that time they changed

10 schools of public affairs where I studied clinical

11 administration and the deliverance of health services.

12   I got a Doctorate at the Hattie Rosenthal School of

13 Psychoanalysis where I got certified many moons ago in

14 psychoanalysis and psychology.

15   After that, my -- well, continuing education and advanced

16 training, I have over a thousand hours at Harvard University,

17 Cambridge Institute and the Department of Psychiatry where I

18 went three times a year and took seminars in family therapy,

19 psychiatry, psychology, and psychoanalysis. I have

20 approximately 60 certificates in that particular field.

21   After that, I -- in conjunction with that, I have about 120

22 hours for the past 15 years at the Ackerman Institute for the

23 Family, which is located in New York City.

24   In addition to that, for certification in psychoanalysis

25 and family therapy, I took approximately 640 hours in my own

6

psychoanalysis. And -- okay.

I am licensed in Georgia in marriage and family therapy.

I am nationally certified in psychology. That's not Georgia. It's a nationally certified accreditation board out of Oklahoma. But my main field is family therapy.

In addition to that, I am a life fellow of the American Psychotherapy Association which evaluates and sets standards for psychotherapists.

I am also a life fellow of the American Orthopsychiatric Association which sets standards for psychiatrists and psychologists. And they -- even though I'm family therapists, I was appointed life fellow after a board went over my credentials for a year.

In addition to that, I have -- Besides that, I have won numerous honors in various fields.

I became the -- Well, I was honored by the American Psychotherapy Association in April of 2016, as a distinguished member, and I received an award and a write-up which went to 30,000 therapists around the country for my work helping dysfunctional families. And I believe you could show all these if you want to, as we go along.

Q   Yes.

A   In addition to that, I have testified on a number of cases. I'll just mention since I was in court on -- I think it was, well, a year and a half ago. 2014 I started on the case

7

1 with you. So 2015, in addition to that I was qualified in about
2 seventy cases.

3 Just recently, a year ago -- well, actually it was ten
4 months ago in Cobb County where the same objections were brought
5 up about, you know, the psychology board and all these things, I
6 was qualified in every field. I think you have a copy of that
7 transcript and the qualifications.

8 I was qualified on numerous occasions in parental
9 alienation, family therapy, family psychology, sexual abuse, and
10 other fields right in Cobb County. I hope I'm not making a
11 mistake on the counties.

12 THE COURT: Sir, let me stop you one second.

13 You're -- You are tendering him as an expert in what
14 field?

15 MS. ████ In family and marriage therapy and the --
16 Yeah. Marriage and family therapist.

17 THE COURT: Okay. Anything else?

18 MS. ████ (No response).

19 THE COURT: As to that --

20 MS. ████ Okay.

21 THE COURT: -- do you have any objection, Ma'am, to
22 him being qualified as an expert in family and marriage
23 therapy?

24 MS. ████ I would have a couple of questions on
25 voir dire.

8

```
 1    THE COURT:  Okay.
 2    MS. ████  Your Honor, can I bring you these for --
 3    THE COURT:  Well, we'll get to that.  Anything other
 4  than family and marriage therapy?
 5    MS. ████  For child -- children at risk --
 6    DR. WEINSTEIN:  Could I --
 7    MS. ████  And --
 8    DR. WEINSTEIN:  Can I state what I --
 9    MS. ████  -- can -- can --
10    DR. WEINSTEIN:  -- state what I testified of?
11    MS. ████  -- Dr. Monty --
12    DR. WEINSTEIN:  No?
13    THE COURT:  No.  No.
14    MS. ████  -- tell what he --
15    THE COURT:  I want to -- I want to know what she --
16    MS. ████  For parental alienation.
17    THE COURT:  -- she wants you to be qualify --
18    THE COURT:  On parental alienation.
19    MS. ████  Uh-huh (affirmative).  Child abuse.
20    THE COURT:  An expert on child abuse?
21    MS. ████  And sexual abuse.
22    THE COURT:  Okay.  All right.
23  I'm -- I'm so sorry.  Is it Ms ████ ?
24    MS. ████ , yes.
25    THE COURT:  Okay.  Ms. ████ , do you want -- have
```

9

```
 1      some voir dire questions?

 2            MS. ███████    Please.

 3            THE COURT:  Go ahead.

 4            MS. ███████       Okay.

 5                        - - -

 6                    VOIR DIRE

 7 BY MS. ███████

 8      Q    When is the last time that you went to a continuing

 9 legal education class?

10      A    Approximately nine months ago at Harvard.

11      Q    And what was that class on?

12      A    In couple therapy.

13      Q    When was the last time that you --

14      A    Oh, also, I'm sorry, at the Ackerman Institute

15 approximately eight months ago on parenting and custodial issues

16 and sex abuse.

17      Q    Okay.  So the name of the continuing education class

18 was parenting --

19      A    Encompassing --

20      Q    -- custodial issues and sex abuse?

21      A    Yes.

22      Q    That was the -- that was the exact name of the

23 seminar?

24      A    I don't know if it was the exact name but I can tell

25 you in 30 seconds.  On my web I have it listed.  So I --

                                                          10
```

```
 1      Q      Where is the Ackerman Institute?

 2      A      Any -- At that time it was East 78th Street.  Now it's

 3 downtown New York City.

 4      Q      Is this an accredited -- a licensed accredited

 5 facility?

 6      A      Yes.  And I went to Harvard every year three times a

 7 year.

 8      Q      When is the last time that you went to a continuing

 9 legal education class in the field of parental alienation?

10      A      At Harvard, but the course was not called parental

11 alienation.  It was called various personalities.

12      Q      Okay.  I'm sorry, sir.  My question was when was the

13 last time?

14      A      Approximately 10 months ago.  And that may be up on my

15 web, too.

16      Q      And you said it was not about parental alienation?

17      A      Well, no, I did not say that.  I said part of the

18 course was parental alienation.

19      Q      When was the last time you attended a CLE on child

20 abuse?

21      A      Approximately --

22      Q      Excuse me, a continuing education course.

23      A      Approximately two years ago in both the Ackerman and

24 Harvard University.

25      Q      And do you maintain a practice?
                                                              11
```

```
 1     A     Yes, I do.

 2     Q     And where is your practice located?

 3     A     It was on 24 East 12th Street in New York City.  I am

 4 now getting another office because the building was just bought

 5 out by a German company just three months ago.

 6     Q     So your practice is located in New York City?

 7     A     For 15 years at 24 East 12th, and also I used an

 8 office here in Alpharetta for a number of years.

 9     Q     How long were you in Alpharetta?  What were the years?

10     A     Approximately 12 years ago 'til now.

11     Q     Okay.  So you maintain an office in Alpharetta?

12     A     I did.  No, I don't.  I maintained an office for 12

13 years.  At this particular time, I'm trying to get another

14 office.  But my office -- I maintained an office and a

15 conference room at Dave Oles' office, which I think I testified

16 last time, who is an attorney.  And I maintained a year before

17 that an office in Forsyth County right across the street from

18 the courthouse.

19     Q     And do you perform forensic evaluations?

20     A     I perform to be exact family assessments.

21     Q     Okay.  And how many family assessments do you perform

22 per year?

23     A     Approximately 200.

24     Q     And is that at your location in Georgia or New York?

25     A     It's all over the country.  All over.  California,
```

                                                                12

```
 1 Colorado, Oklahoma, New Jersey.

 2     Q    How many cases have you been -- have you not been

 3 qualified as an expert in?

 4     A    Maybe one case.

 5     Q    Maybe one case?

 6     A    Yes.

 7     Q    There could be more?

 8     A    Yes.  One case.

 9     Q    And when was that case?

10     A    That was three years ago on a -- where they were

11 looking for another individual.  I wasn't even in the courtroom.

12 This was in District Court --

13     Q    And where is that -- where was that case?

14     A    Well, that was in -- in court in New York City.

15     Q    Are you the subject of any malpractice litigation?

16     A    No, I'm not.

17          MS. ███████    Your Honor, may I submit his licensing

18     and --

19          THE COURT:  Well, yeah.  Whatever you want me to see,

20     you need to let Ms. ███████████ see first, okay?

21          MS. ██████    Okay.

22          THE COURT:  So just go ahead and gather up --

23          MS. ██████    All right.

24          THE COURT:  -- whatever you want to show me and then

25     hand it to her.

                                                              13
```

```
 1        MS. ███████  Okay.

 2        THE COURT:  All right, Doctor, you're -- you're

 3   requested to be accepted as an expert in the fields of

 4   family and marriage therapy, parental alienation --

 5        DR. WEINSTEIN:  Should I --

 6        THE COURT:  -- child abuse, and sexual abuse.  Do you

 7   consider yourself an expert in those fields?

 8        THE WITNESS:  I -- Yes, I do.  I've testified in those

 9   fields.

10        THE COURT:  And in terms of child abuse and sexual

11   abuse, I guess we could be more specific.  You consider

12   yourself to be an expert in the psychological aspects of

13   child abuse and sexual abuse?

14        THE WITNESS:  I do, even though I'm not a Georgia

15   psychologist.

16        THE COURT:  All right.  All right.

17        DR. WEINSTEIN:  And --

18        THE COURT:  I will accept Dr. Weinstein as an expert

19   in family and marriage therapy, parental alienation, and

20   the psychological aspects of child and sexual abuse.  Any

21   shortcomings which Ms. ███████ may or may not believe

22   that he has will go to the weight, but I'll let him testify

23   as an expert.

24        MS. ██████  Okay.  May I give you these now?

25        THE COURT:  Do you have any objection to me seeing
```

                                                              14

     1 | those, Ms. ███████████

     2 | MS. ███████████   I'm sorry. I'm still reviewing them.

     3 | THE COURT: Okay. Ma'am, if you could just --

     4 | THE WITNESS: May I have some water?

     5 | THE COURT: Can you have water?

     6 | DR. WEINSTEIN: Yes. I'm sorry.

     7 | THE COURT: I don't mind at all. I just -- What I'll

     8 | do is I will ask my assistant to bring some in.

     9 | DR. WEINSTEIN: Thank you.

    10 | THE COURT: I'll just shoot her a text.

    11 | DR. WEINSTEIN: Thank you.

    12 | THE COURT: Ma'am, if you want to just put those aside

    13 | for the moment to give ███████████ --

    14 | MS. ██████ Okay.

    15 | THE COURT: -- a chance to see them.

    16 | And, Mr. ██████ have you seen them?

    17 | MR. ██████   I have, Judge.

    18 | THE COURT: Okay. And then you can ahead with your

    19 | questioning.

    20 | MS. ██████   Okay.

    21 | DIRECT EXAMINATION

    22 | BY MS. ██████: (Resumed)

    23 | Q   All right. Dr. Weinstein, when was the first time

    24 | that I contacted you? Around what time frame did you see my

    25 | children for the first time?

                                                                    15

1   A   It was approximately March, 2014.

 2   Q   And at that time -- I have a report that you wrote,

 3 and in the report at this time you stated that --

 4   DR. WEINSTEIN: I'm sorry. I still need a little

 5   water.

 6   THE COURT: I'm asking for it.

 7   DR. WEINSTEIN: Oh, fine. Thank you. Forgive me.

 8 BY MS. ███████ (Resuming)

 9   Q   You stated I am here at a very heartbreaking moment

10 because her son ████████ has not seen █████ for nine months.

11 Today he was supposed to come for her birthday and he did not

12 show up. And according to this -- this was on March 23rd, 2014

13 -- you also wrote that ████████ --

14   THE COURT: Is this a question, Ma'am?

15   MS. ████████   I'm -- I'm going to ask a question --

16   THE COURT: You're going to ask a question?

17   MS. ████████   -- Your Honor.

18   THE COURT: Okay.

19   MS. ████████   Okay.

20   THE COURT: Ask the question.

21   MS. ████████   Okay.

22 BY MS. ███████ (Resuming)

23   Q   So from your observation at the time, in your opinion,

24 do you consider ████████ was being alienated?

25   A   When I saw -- First of all, I didn't see ████████ when

                                                              16

```
 1  I first --
 2        MS. ███████      Your Honor, I'd object to relevance.
 3  This is based upon a question that happened in 2014.
 4        MS. ███████   It's relevant, Your Honor.
 5        THE COURT:  All right. And you believe it's irrelevant
 6  because it's, what?  Before the divorce I'm guessing?
 7        MS. ███████    Precisely.  He -- he was an expert
 8  that was hired in the divorce action, and all of this would
 9  have been subsequent to the incident action that we're here
10  today for.
11        MS. ███████  Your Honor, this was actually right before
12  the order was written up, so it has relevance in this since
13  ███████ filed the divorce July of 2012 --
14        THE COURT:  All right.
15        MS. ███████  And then we had a temporary --
16        THE COURT:  Well, you know, there's two issues in a
17  modification of custody.  One is whether there's been a
18  material -- material change in circumstances since the last
19  order.
20        The other one is best interest.
21        And so I think I can go beyond, or behind, the date of
22  the last order to consider best interest.
23        And also, if I'm going to figure out whether there's
24  been a change in circumstances, I need to understand what
25  the circumstances were at that time.
```

17

1   So I overrule your objection.

2   MS. ███████   And, Your Honor, again just for the

3   record that the court at the time definitively ruled that

4   there was no parental alienation in the divorce decree.

5   THE COURT: Okay.

6   MS. █████   Dr. Monty was not involved at that time --

7   THE COURT: Let's keep --

8   MS. █████   -- and I was --

9   THE COURT: Let's keep moving.

10   MS. █████   Okay. Okay.

11 BY MS. █████   (Resuming)

12   Q   So, in your opinion, was ████████ alienated from me

13 especially not coming to my birthday?

14   A   Yes. I spent about ten hours with you. I spoke to

15 █████ and I spoke to everyone in your family, and I was looking

16 forward to at least observing you, not probing, observing you

17 with █████

18   I wrote down -- and I don't have that in front of me. I

19 don't like to read papers in front of me -- that █████ has not

20 seen you before 2014 on numerous, numerous occasions.

21   He refused to come to your birthday. He spent -- I don't

22 believe he spent any time with you during Christmas. There was

23 no real parenting time and there was nothing -- I went through

24 the papers late at night after I spent time with you and your

25 family and I was trying to figure out what the Court or █████

                                                        18

1 is hanging his hat on.

2   Why should he not visit with you, which I believe is -- was

3 a loving, nurturing, caring mother and a grandmother that was

4 nurturing and an aunt that was nurturing and an extended family

5 that was very cooperative with me during this interplay.

6   So there was no -- I believe there was the beginning of

7 alienation, but I didn't come to a full conclusion yet because I

8 went back a number of times to observe -- try -- excuse me, try

9 to observe ████████ in his relationship with you and also try to

10 observe ██████ again for a period of time.

11   THE COURT: Ms. ██████ I'm not telling you you can't

12   ask him these questions, but I will tell you what I'm most

13   interested in --

14   MS. ██████ Okay.

15   THE COURT: -- is what has happened since the divorce.

16   MS. ██████ Okay.

17   THE COURT: I'm interested in that.

18   MS. ██████ Okay.

19 BY MS. ██████ (Resuming)

20   Q   Dr. Monty, I have three reports here where you have

21 visited me with my children. The lastest was actually -- it was

22 -- I'll just get it from the back forward.

23   MS. ██████ Your Honor, I'd object to the form of

24   the question.

25   THE COURT: All right. Well, I'll let her finish and

                                                              19

```
 1        we'll see what the question is.
 2 BY MS. ████████   (Resuming)
 3        Q     March of 2016, the 17th -- Dr. Monty, do you recognize
 4 this?
 5             THE COURT:  Show Ms. ████████████ first, please, before
 6        you show the witness.
 7             MS. ██████  Okay.
 8             THE COURT:  Mr. ████████ you're just going to have to
 9        shout out when you need to see something.
10             MR. ████████  That's fine, Judge.  I believe the
11        plaintiff has provided me with all of these.
12             THE COURT:  Okay.
13             MR. ████████  But if I haven't seen something, I will
14        shout out.
15             THE COURT:  All right.
16             MS. ██████  Was there any objection on the license for
17        evidence?
18             THE COURT:  Just give her one minute.
19                            - - -
20             (Whereupon, Ms. ████████████ was reviewing documents.)
21                            - - -
22             MS. ██████████  Here you go.
23             THE COURT:  All right.  Ms. ████████████, those initial
24        documents concerning the doctor's qualifications, do you
25        have any objection to me seeing those documents?
                                                                  20
```

1   MS. ██████████: No, Your Honor.

2   THE COURT: All right. So those will come into

3 evidence.

4   MS. ██████ Okay.

5   THE COURT: Ma'am, you've got them together as a

6 group. Why don't you -- You're marking that as what?

7   MS. ██████: Exhibit 1.

8   THE COURT: All right. Let's make it P-1.

9   MS. ██████: P-1.

10   THE COURT: P for plaintiff, okay?

11   MS. ██████ Okay.

12   THE COURT: Now are those the doctor's certificates?

13   MS. ██████: This is Dr. Monty's resume.

14   THE COURT: Okay. You can just hand it to me.

15   MS. ██████: Okay.

16   THE COURT: The whole thing together.

17   MS. ██████ Okay. And then this one is his license

18 for Georgia.

19   THE COURT: I'll look through it. There's no

20 objection, so --

21   MS. ██████ Okay.

22   THE COURT: -- this is -- all has to do with the

23 Doctor; right?

24   MS. ██████ Yes.

25   THE COURT: All right. So P-1 is admitted without

21

```
 1  objection.

 2                        - - -

 3        (Whereupon, Plaintiff's Exhibit 1 was tendered and

 4     admitted without objection into evidence.)

 5                        - - -

 6        THE COURT:  Now there is some other documents you were

 7     about to show him.  You can go ahead and show him.

 8        MS. ████    Yes.

 9  BY MS. ████    (Resuming)

10     Q    Dr. Monty, did you recognize this report that you did

11  in 2016?

12     A    Forgive me.  (Reviewing) I just want to be sure what

13  this is.  Yes, this is my report of many.  It's part of one

14  giant report.

15     Q    So when you wrote this report back in March of 2016,

16  what was your -- in your opinion, what was going on with the

17  children at that time?

18     A    Well, first of all, I based my report on a number of

19  observations.  I based my report on observing ████ with his

20  children.  I based my report on speaking to little ████  I

21  based my report on the amount of time ████ was seeing you,

22  and I based my report on some research which was done where

23  there was some -- every venue has a different -- on -- corporal

24  punishment against ████   and I felt that the children because

25  of the temperament, your personality, would be best living with

                                                            22
```

1 you.

2   They were very well behaved. I believe they could be very

3 well behaved together, that ███████ has certain issues that has

4 to be worked on, but without getting psychobabble, it was not a

5 causal effect.

6   The fact that ████████ is acting out now did not come to a

7 quick metamorphosis the minute you took over. It came through a

8 number of years of whatever with his father, and his father is,

9 in my opinion, which I mentioned there based on what I observed

10 and how he related to me, maybe a little bit more aggressive

11 than most people that I deal with, and so I felt that the

12 children would be -- would grow and develop and mature on -- in

13 your custody.

14   I also felt -- which I'm not sure this -- I didn't read the

15 whole report quickly because I don't like to be a rote

16 memorization, but you were constantly studying therapeutic

17 techniques and techniques the best way to bring up children

18 going through a contentious divorce.

19   I believe you're even becoming a licensed therapist or

20 studying that in graduate school, and I believe you had a very

21 strong -- since I teach in colleges -- you have very strong

22 insight and feeling, okay, for children at risk, and that's why

23 I also -- so I wouldn't just take my word which my report was.

24 I believe it's the other report coming down. I -- I called in a

25 person that works with me who's from Harvard for children at

                                                          23

```
 1 | risk.

 2 |         MS. ███████████:  Your Honor, I object to eliciting

 3 |    narrative.  I'm not sure where the question and the answer

 4 |    -- the answer started or began.

 5 |         THE COURT:  All right.  Are you done with the answer?

 6 |         DR. WEINSTEIN:  Yes.

 7 |         THE COURT:  All right.

 8 |         MS. ███████:  Okay.

 9 |         THE COURT:  Overruled.

10 | BY MS. ████████   (Resuming)

11 |    Q    From this report where you encountered ███████████--

12 |         MS. ████████  And actually this is a picture, Your

13 |    Honor, that I would like to submit as evidence of ██████

14 |    █████████, and this is those --

15 |         MS. ███████████:  Your Honor, I object to improper

16 |    foundation.

17 |         THE COURT:  Okay.  Well, before you can show a witness

18 |    anything or show me --

19 |         MS. ███████  Oh.

20 |         THE COURT:  -- in fairness you got to let the opposing

21 |    counsel see it so she will be on the same page and know

22 |    what you're talking to me about.

23 |         MS. ████████  Okay.

24 |         THE COURT:  All right now.  You have a picture.

25 |         THE COURT:  And let's mark it.

                                                              24
```

1   MS. ███████: Okay.

2   THE COURT: Just for identification. And it is -- if

3   you're going in order, I guess that'd be P-2. And go ahead

4   and tell me what you want to tell me about it before I look

5   at it.

6   MS. ███████: Okay. This is a picture of my oldest son

7   ███████, and this is a picture of the girl who accused him

8   of sexual battery. They had been dating since 2012.

9   THE COURT: Well, are you testifying now? Just tell

10   me --

11   MS. ██████ Okay.

12   THE COURT: Tell me what it is. All right.

13   MS.'██████ Okay.

14   THE COURT: You want me to admit P-2 into evidence; is

15   that right?

16   MS.██████ Correct.

17   THE COURT: Okay.

18   MS. ████████   And, Your Honor, I object. It's an

19   improper foundation.

20   THE COURT: All right.

21   MS. █████ This --

22   THE COURT: You have --

23   MS. █████ Okay.

24   THE COURT: You have not laid the proper foundation,

25   so I sustain the objection. You can try again if you want.

                                                              25

```
 1        MS. ████  Okay.  So this is a picture of ██████
 2   with his girlfriend at the Magnolia Plantation where Dr.
 3   Monty was present to observe.
 4        THE COURT:  Well --
 5        MS. ████████  Your Honor, again, I'm objecting to
 6   improper foundation and testify -- to testifying --
 7   testimony while --
 8        THE COURT:  Okay.
 9        MS. ████████  -- you have a witness on the stand on
10   direct.
11        THE COURT:  All right.
12        Ms. ████  I'm -- I'm more of a referee.  I can't take
13   your side.  I can't take --
14        MS. ████  Right.
15      ·  THE COURT:  -- the other side, and I can't tell you
16   how to do it, but right now you're not doing it right.
17        MS. ████  Okay.
18        THE COURT:  And so I sustain the objection.
19        MS. ████  Okay.  Can I -- About this report --
20        THE COURT:  You can hand it to him and ask a question,
21   and if there's an objection, I guess we'll hear it.
22 BY MS. ████  (Resuming)
23   Q    Dr. Monty, do you recognize that report, and do you
24 recognize this picture?
25   A    May I just review this to make sure I have the right
                                                          26
```

```
 1 report (reviewing).
 2       MS. ██████████   Your Honor, I haven't seen the report.
 3   I saw a picture.
 4       THE COURT:  I thought that was the same -- it's the
 5   same --
 6       MS. ██████   It's the same.
 7       THE COURT:  Is that the same report you showed her
 8   earlier?
 9       MS. ██████:  Yeah.
10       THE COURT:  Okay.
11       MS. ████████   Okay.
12       DR. WEINSTEIN:  It -- it's my report.  I just wanted
13   to see the report to be sure.  Forgive me.
14 BY MS. ██████   (Resuming)
15   Q    Okay.  In this report, this is -- you -- you wrote in
16 this report while I accompanied Ms. ██████ to Magnolia House, a
17 public building in Powder Springs --
18       MS. ████████   Your Honor, I object -- She may ask
19   questions about his report or have him recall that rather
20   than reading a narrative into the record.
21       THE COURT:  Okay.  Ma'am, are you tendering that
22   report into evidence?
23       MS. ██████   Yes, sir.
24       THE COURT:  Okay.  Do you have any objection to the
25   report?
```
27

```
 1          MS. ████████    Let me make sure.  If I could take one

 2    quick look at that?  (Reviewing) Your Honor, I would object

 3    on the -- on the basis of relevance, the report from

 4    Friday, May 2nd, 2014, well before the parties were

 5    divorced.

 6          MS. ██████   Your Honor, this establishes the type of

 7    demeanor of --

 8          THE COURT:  Go ahead and mark it.

 9          MS. ████████  --   ██████████  --

10          THE COURT:  Go ahead and mark it.  Is that P-3, Ma'am?

11          MS. ████████   Yes, sir.

12          THE COURT:  Okay.  All right.  And you're offering it

13    because -- for what purpose?

14          MS. ██████    I -- I did want to ask Dr. Monty has he

15    ever -- ever had an altercation with ████████████ and it --

16    it was direct --

17          THE COURT:  Were you offering it for any other purpose

18    other than about the altercation?

19          MS. ███████    To show that -- what was said about

20    ████████ in here and his observations.

21          THE COURT:  All right.  I'll -- I'll admit the report

22    into evidence.  I'll reassure the parties and Ms. ██████████

23    that the order says what it says, and I'm not

24    second-guessing the previous order.  So I've got the report

25    as P-3 in evidence.

                                                              28
```

1   P-2 I don't believe has been tendered into evidence,
2   or if it has --
3   MS. ███████ No, sir.
4   THE COURT: All right. So P-2 is admitted. I mean --
5   I'm sorry. P-3, the report is admitted.
6   The photograph has not been tendered and is not
7   admitted.
8   - - -
9   (Whereupon, Plaintiff's Exhibit P-3 was tendered and
10   admitted into evidence.)
11   - - -
12   MS. ████████ Can we admit the -- let's see, did we get
13   this first one -- the first report admitted into evidence?
14   And there's three total that I want to admit into
15   evidence.
16   THE COURT: All I have is P-3 which is dated May 2,
17   2014.
18   MS. ███████ Okay. And this one is March, 2016. I'd
19   like to tender this one into evidence.
20   THE COURT: Show Ms. ████████████
21   MS. ███████ This is another one that was in that pile.
22   MS. █████████ (Reviewing.)
23   MS. ███████ And I'd also like to tender into
24   evidence --
25   THE COURT: All right. Your -- the other report is
                                                              29

```
 1    what?  Marked as what?

 2        MS. ████████:  This one is the very first one that Dr.

 3    Monty did.  His first review.

 4        THE COURT:  Which is the one that you showed Ms.

 5    █████████?

 6        MS. ██████  This was the --

 7        THE COURT:  Okay.  It's marked --

 8        MS. ██████  March --

 9        THE COURT:  It's marked as what?

10        MS. ██████  P-3

11        MS. ████████:  Four.

12        MS. ██████  P-4.

13        THE COURT:  Okay.  Any objection to P-4?

14        MS. ████████  There's been no foundation laid for

15    anything about the report.

16        THE COURT:  All right.  I'm going to give you back

17    P-2.  That's not in evidence.

18    MS. ██████  Okay.

19        THE COURT:  P-4 the objection was there is no

20    foundation.  So I will sustain the objection and give this

21    back to you, as well.

22        MS. ██████  All right.

23 BY MS. ██████  (Resuming)

24    Q   In your opinion, Dr. Monty, with what is going on --

25 with what you have seem, for a child to be -- How would a child
```
                                                                    30

1 act out after being constrained [sic] for two years --

2   MS. ▮▮▮▮▮▮▮ Your Honor, objection. Leading the

3   witness.

4   THE COURT: Overruled.

5   DR. WEINSTEIN: If a child, in my opinion, based on

6   research in the years that I've spent in this -- if a child

7   is restrained for a number of years, it leads to what is

8   called a frustration aggression hypothesis, either fight or

9   flight. Either they run away as you see so many children

10   today running away or they act out in many different ways.

11   I'm predicating that on my research, on my writings,

12   and my years of working with dysfunctional families and

13   children. So children that are restrained in many cases --

14   it's not all cases -- in many cases, usually act out in

15   socially maladjusted ways.

16   And I can go into the research on it but you didn't

17   ask me that.

18 BY MS. ▮▮▮▮▮ (Resuming)

19   Q So in them acting out, in your opinion, would a

20 rebellious child acting out against authority, would that be

21 part of it?

22   A Yes.

23   Q In your opinion, a child doing poorly in school, would

24 that be part of it?

25   A Yes.

1   Q   In your opinion, a child who is depressed, would that
2 be part of it?

3   A   Not necessarily. Depression is a symptom, helpless
4 anger if there's no chemical pathology such as in bipolar and
5 schizophrenia. So the answer to that particular question is
6 yes, you know. Yes, but I have to break it down.

7   Depression is not a catalyst for acting out. There are
8 other forms of how depressed personalities act out, and there
9 are different forms of depressed personalities.

10   So it's yes and no to the answer, and if it's pathological
11 schizophrenia, that would not be part of your answer. If it's
12 an environmental situation, then it can be part of the
13 situation. Many adolescents act out because they are in a
14 situation of helpless anger.

15   Q   In your opinion on this case, what is your observation
16 of ███████

17   A.   Could you just tell me time, date and place? Are you
18 talking about May 2nd observation or are you talking about
19 recently or --

20   Q   Well, we'll start with the May 2nd where Mr. ███████ was
21 also there -- the interaction.

22   MS. ███████   And Your Honor, I'd just ask -- if I
23   may clarify -- May 2nd of what year are we discussing?

24   THE COURT: Yeah, please clarify.

25 BY MS. ███████   (Resuming)

                                                          32

1   Q   May 2nd of 2014.

2   A   May I just see that to refresh my memory? I want to

3 make sure I have the exact time, date and place to answer the

4 question.

5   Q   Yes.

6   A   (Reviewing) ███████ was acting out as the basis of

7 feeling frustrated and a feeling of being in his mind rejected

8 and a feeling of not being a participant, and he did not show

9 during that time, and this was at anecdotal periods of time, he

10 was very hostile to you during those periods. The baseball game

11 and the period prior to that where he didn't come over, and the

12 acting out was a different format.

13   Q   Could that be caused by parental alienation?

14   A   That is one aspect of parental alienation. Parent --

15 The alienated child acts out in many ways. There is divided

16 loyalty and confusion and that's part of a symptomology

17 predicated upon what thought, you know, what thinking you were

18 doing in order to identify it.

19   Yes parental alienation exists. That was part of it and

20 subsequently ██████ was -- was a victim of that alienation in

21 particular during a great period of time, at least two years,

22 when you didn't have real contact with him. That was part of

23 the acting out. That was part of what phenomenon of parental

24 alienation was. He was a victim of parental alienation.

25   Q   Okay. Let's move on to ██████ The last time that you

1 saw ███████, could you give the Court your opinion on the

2 situation with him.

3   A   I saw ███████ for several -- for at least a year and a

4 half. During three visits -- ███████ was very tied to you. He

5 was very close to you. He did not do anything without your

6 consent. He was very polite. I found him to be extremely

7 intelligent, very aware of what was going on. You presented a

8 number of things to him. You took him to games, in the old

9 house. You took him to the park. You sat there and worked with

10 him and his homework, and I observed then ███████ was -- was

11 looking upon you not only as, quote-unquote, an authority figure

12 but was looking to you with love, nurturing, and warmth. And I

13 -- he's just a wonderful kid and both parents should be proud.

14   Q   In your opinion -- where no evidence has been proven

15 -- could your -- could you give your opinion of me as a mother?

16   A   Okay. I find you to be a warm, bonding, nurturing

17 mother, a mother that works, a mother that's struggling, a

18 mother that is up against great odds. You keep your house much

19 cleaner than I keep mine. You are very neat. You have

20 everything in order. You read to the children.

21   You bring books in. You try to do all the research in

22 therapy and child psychology and all those aspects. I have

23 never seen in my 20 hours I observed you scream at the children,

24 and I find in an overall -- overall mommy evaluation, you are in

25 -- you are a very kind, loving mother that puts the children

                                                              34

1 before anyone.

2   Q   Okay. In your opinion on let's say ▓▓▓▓ now. With

3 the move and an eight-year old seeing -- or nine-year old seeing

4 his mother four days a month, what, in your opinion, would that

5 have an effect on him

6   A   ▓▓▓▓ --

7   Q   -- becoming bonded?

8   A   ▓▓▓▓ is a nine-year old boy. When I saw him in

9 intense -- was seeing him, he was like eight and seven and a

10 half. The fact that he only sees you for four days would have

11 down the road a devastating affect such as endocapresis

12 (phonetic), separation anxiety and a number of things, because

13 he was -- When I saw him was very extremely bonded with you, and

14 the fact that he does not have an ongoing relationship with you

15 and to a degree with ▓▓▓▓, all right, has down the road would

16 have a devastating affect on him, such as panic anxiety,

17 separation anxiety, endocapresis (phonetic). And there's a

18 great deal of studies just on that of children being ripped

19 away.

20   Q   In your opinion, do you think ▓▓▓▓ the older son,

21 the two years he was away from me has an effect on his behavior

22 now?

23   A   Yes.

24   Q   From you interaction with Mr. ▓▓▓▓ do you see, in

25 your opinion, any flexibility with his actions and co-parenting

35

1 skills?

2   A   I have never been a co-parent therapist to Mr. ████

3 or to yourself. But as far as his skills, the way he came off

4 to me that day in my face telling me to get out, in public,

5 where I was just docile and passive, and his threat to an

6 individual who works with me, in terms of I'm going to sue you

7 and all these other things, I don't think that's in the best

8 interest of any of the children, and that plays a role towards

9 his personality.

10   Q   Okay. Have you ever been encountered by Mr. ████

11   A   Yeah, he told me to get out, move out, stay away from

12 his children, and I wasn't even near his child. And I could

13 deal with that, I could look at it clinically, but I thought --

14 I thought that was a bit inappropriate.

15   Q   So, in your opinion, should ████ and ████ be

16 separated?

17   A   In my opinion, I do not believe that ████ or ████

18 should be separated even though ████ has been acting out in a

19 number of situations, ████ still loves him. ████ looks at him

20 as a big brother, and I believe ████ needs ████ and ████

21 needs ████ and I believe, you know, separating siblings during

22 unfortunately contentious divorce is not a healthy thing.

23   And there was a great deal of research done on that and I

24 can take up if you wanted to go into the work of people who were

25 torn away and broken up families. The Judge is very aware of

36

1 all this -- what the issue is. But it's -- it's not in this

2 particular case a healthy factor for them to be separated in my

3 opinion.

4   Q   In your opinion, what would be the best scenario for

5 those boys?

6   A   In my opinion, the best scenario would be that number

7 one that they live with you, that they have -- that you raise

8 them, that you foster a relationship, that the father has

9 liberal parenting time, that the father is in the picture, that

10 they know that this is the father, that they see him, and have a

11 relationship.

12   I think the entire family would benefit from an independent

13 family therapist or family psychologist that can work with them

14 on dealing with issues such as anger and personality and

15 focusing on the importance of how they behave, because a family

16 therapist is really trained to see how they behave has a

17 residual affect on the children.

18   And with, you know, ███████ -- I believe, yes, he has to have

19 some, I hate to swear, forgive me, anger management to deal more

20 appropriately on how he deals with certain aspects of anger.

21   Q   Thank you, Dr. Monty.

22   THE COURT: Cross?

23   - - -

24   CROSS-EXAMINATION

25 BY MS. ███████

                                                    37

```
 1     Q    Dr. Monty, you've never had an appointment with ████
 2 ████  correct?
 3     A    I tried to make one.
 4     Q    You've never had an appointment with ████████?
 5     A    The answer is yes, correct.
 6     Q    Okay.  And in fact, the only time that you ever saw
 7 ████████  was when you ambushed at a baseball field with his
 8 children; right?
 9     A    Can't answer that question.  I didn't ambush him.
10     Q    Okay.
11     A    That's a derogative -- I don't ambush people except
12 when I was in the service.
13     Q    So your interaction and you seeing ████████ was at a
14 baseball field; correct?
15     A    Correct.
16     Q    And you had not contacted ████████ prior to coming to
17 this baseball field in Dallas, Georgia; correct?
18     A    I can't recall.
19     Q    Okay.  Anyways, this -- how long ago did that happen?
20     A    Two years ago.
21     Q    Okay.  And that -- two years ago, and that was your
22 sole interaction with him; correct?
23     A    What do you mean sole interaction?
24     Q    You going to the baseball field and seeing ████████
25 Have you had any other interactions with ████████ apart from
                                                              38
```

1 that day at the baseball field?

2   A   No. I have not.

3   Q   Okay. And you showed up and started talking to the

4 kids without even consulting ███████; isn't that right?

5   A   When are we speaking about?

6   Q   At the baseball field in 2014.

7   A   No. The answer is no.

8   Q   Okay.

9   A   I observed the children.

10   Q   And it --

11   A   And after -- and I'll give you the exact scenario.

12 When Mr. ██████ said get out, you know, and get out of here and

13 whatever he said afterwards, I went -- I looked at the baseball

14 game because that was interesting, and then I went to Ms.

15 ██████ s car and sat down.

16   Q   So you were invited to the baseball game by Ms. ██████

17 is that right?

18   A   Yes, I was.

19   Q   And Ms. ██████ wasn't present in the stadium or sitting

20 in the bleachers at the time you approached the children, was

21 she?

22   A   I didn't approach the children. Didn't we just say

23 that?

24   Q   Okay. And, again, this is during the course of an

25 ongoing divorce; correct?

39

```
 1    A    I believe so, yes.

 2    Q    You haven't seen -- Have you diagnosed ██████ with

 3 any sort of behavioral health issue?

 4    A    I did not diagnose him per se.  I made an assessment

 5 of how he interacts with other members of the family, in

 6 particular the mother, and --

 7    Q    So that would be no.

 8    A    -- and that was predicated on -- can I finish the

 9 answer?

10    Q    Certainly.

11    A    And that was predicated on my observations, me

12 speaking to Ms. ██████ looking at the court records afterwards,

13 and also speaking to my associate who made -- who saw both

14 children up 'til now, and I spoke to her in depth.  And in

15 addition to that, I read a report.  I don't know if it was

16 submitted or not that she wrote.  And I did speak to ██████

17 over the phone a week ago.  I was in Georgia, and I said -- I

18 asked him would you like -- I tried to make an --

19         MS. ██████    Your Honor, I object to any hearsay

20    testimony.

21         THE COURT:  All right.  Don't tell us what someone

22    else said, please, sir.

23         DR. WEINSTEIN:  Okay.

24 BY MS. ██████    (Resuming)

25    Q    What did you review to -- the documents you reviewed
                                                          40
```

```
 1  in preparation of your testimony today?

 2       A    What is my review of my documents?

 3       Q    What documents have you reviewed --

 4       A    I read Karen Wagners report.

 5       Q    -- in preparation for your testimony today?

 6       A    I spoke to the children.  I spoke to Ms. ██████████

 7  I spoke -- I mentioned that -- to ████████████████, and that's

 8  what I reviewed.

 9       Q    And when did you speak to ███████?

10       A    I spoke to ████████ October 21st and October 22nd over

11  the phone, and ████████.

12       Q    And what telephone number did you call to speak with

13  them?

14       A    I -- I can't recall what telephone number.

15       Q    Did you --

16       A    I don't even know my number.

17       Q    -- call Ms. ████████

18       A    I spoke to Ms. ████████    Correct.

19       Q    Okay.

20       A    In fact -- please forgive me -- I had Ms. ██████ come

21  and see me where I was in the conference room, and I asked her

22  for the number.  That's what I did.

23       Q    Okay.  So Ms. ████████ was physically present with you

24  and you spoke to the boys for a few minutes on the phone in

25  October.
```

```
 1       A    No.  She wasn't.  I walked away when I was speaking to
 2  the boys.
 3       Q    Okay.  Prior to that, how often has -- Excuse me --
 4  Let me back that up.  ██████  has never come to visit you at the
 5  office since August of 2015, has he?
 6       A    No.
 7       Q    Okay.  And --
 8       A    I'm not his therapist.  It would be inappropriate.
 9       Q    Okay.  And ██████ has not physically seen you since
10  2014; correct?
11       A    They both have not --- No.  It was 2015, I believe.
12  And --
13       Q    When in 2015?
14       A    I -- I can't recall.  That's why I have to look at the
15  reports.  It'll give you an exact time, date and place of when
16  they physically interacted with me.  So what I did, if you want
17  to call, I spoke to them.  I didn't physically interact with
18  them.  I didn't feel that was appropriate.
19       Q    Okay.  Now you went on at length discussing the
20  problems with children who are alienated from one parent, and
21  that they would act out.  And that would be if -- to quantify
22  that testimony, is that if they are held from the other parent
23  beyond their will?
24       A    Forgive me, I don't understand what --
25       Q    Certainly.
```

```
 1    A    -- you're saying.

 2    Q    Certainly.  You testified -- you testified that

 3 children who are alienated from one parent manifest a host of

 4 problems including acting out; correct?

 5    A    That's part of it, depending upon the case, depending

 6 upon the alienation, depending upon the severity of the

 7 alienation, depending upon a number of phenomena, many of them

 8 act out.  Many of them repress their anger.  Many of them fall

 9 into frustration aggression hypotheses and many of them have

10 difficulty later on relating, because they don't know who to

11 identify with, and there's no bonding.

12    Q    Yet --

13    A    Yes there is -- in answer -- I'm ready for the answer.

14 And yes, there is acting out many times where children that have

15 been alienated.

16    Q    Okay.  There's acting out.  So if that child is now

17 put with a parent that they were supposedly alienated from, do

18 we expect that acting out to increase in measure and scope and

19 frequency?

20    A    If -- Let me -- Could I just ask the question to

21 myself?  If children are put back with the alienated parent,

22 with the parent that's perpetrating the alienation, would they

23 still continue to act out?

24    Q    No.

25    A    Is that the question?
```

43

```
1      Q    Let me back this up, and I'll be very deliberate.   If
2   a child who allegedly was alienated from a parent, Parent A, is
3   now back in the custody of Parent A, do you expect for that
4   child's behavior, the acting out incidents, to increase with
5   frequency and aggression and severity?
6      A    Okay.  If they are put back with the alienator,
7   without going into particulars, then the probability factor is
8   strong that they are acting out would increase with Parent A.
9      Q    Okay.  So the parent they were alienated -- supposedly
10  alienated from, being placed back in their --
11     A    That's a different question.
12     Q    Okay.
13     A    The parents that they are alienated from are Parent B.
14  So Parent A is the alienator.
15     Q    So let me --
16     A    -- according to what you're saying.
17     Q    -- just put this in real terms.
18          THE COURT:  I think he --
19          MS. ███████:  -- Ms. ████ alleges --
20          THE COURT:  -- misunderstood your question.
21          MS. ███████:  Okay.
22          THE COURT:  I think he misunderstood your question.
23      Her question was using Parent A -- Parent A is the
24      alienator, Parent B the child is really not getting to see
25      because he's alienated from that parent.  So her question
                                                              44
```

1   was if the child who has been in the custody of Parent A is

2   then placed with Parent B, would you expect the scope and

3   magnitude of the acting out to increase?

4   Was that your question?

5   DR. WEINSTEIN: No, this is clear. It would decrease.

6   THE COURT: Was that your question?

7   MS. ███████   Yes.

8   THE COURT: Okay.

9   DR. WEINSTEIN: It would decrease if it's put back to

10   Parent B according to the way Your Honor describes.

11 MS. ███████:   (Resuming)

12   Q   So then what would your opinion be of the fact that

13 since ███████ has been in Ms. ███████ s custody from August of

14 2015 to now, he not only has amassed a quite impressive criminal

15 record as well as being suspended from school and continues to

16 be truant to the point of parents being notified by the state?

17 What would be your opinion of that?

18   A   My opinion is, and I am trying not to be psychobabble.

19 So forgive me. It's not the causal affect relationship. It's

20 called the theory of concomitant variations. There are many

21 issues of why children act out years and five years later.

22   Children develop as they become adults. Panic anxiety, the

23 -- the histrionic embracing the anger for years before, the

24 empirical validity of how they acted out comes years later.

25   So what is happening in this particular case is ███████ is

                                                                   45

now acting out because the seeds of confusion, hysteria, and
acting out behavior based on what I think is going on, he is
manifesting some of his father's behavior of acting out during a
period of time. So if they act out when they are with mommy,
that doesn't mean mommy created this pathology all at once in
the past year. This -- the seeds of this pathology were created
years earlier.

I am not saying that ████ is the only factor of why an
adolescent acts out. I am not saying ████ is the reason why
there all ills in the world. But what I am saying is just
because it happens in the custody of the parent, that doesn't
mean causal affect that that parent created this phenomena all
at once. The phenomena is created during the impressionable
years. So my opinion is based on a number of things and a
number of mental health experts that have spent all their life
in a laboratory.

Q   So do you find it sufficient in your expert opinion to
base a parental opinion -- Excuse me -- an opinion on someone's
parenting on less than an hour at a baseball field of
observation?

MS. ████   Objection. There was more than one hour
according to the reports.

MS. ████   And, Your Honor, I would respond that
my earlier question when I asked him about where he
observed --

46

```
 1           THE COURT:  Well, just ask the question.  The doctor
 2      is capable of correcting any built-in falsehoods in the
 3      question, if there are any.
 4           MS. ███████████  Okay.
 5 BY MS. ███████████  (Resuming)
 6      Q    So in your expert opinion, it is standard practice to
 7 make a parenting opinion on observations of someone for one hour
 8 of time at a public event?
 9      A    The answer is no.  It's the amount -- the amount of
10 time that you can do -- the more time the better.  However, that
11 is not what I did.  I made an opinion on an acting out behavior
12 of an adult towards me where I felt menaced.  And then I related
13 that, how would a child that is nine years old or fourteen feel
14 if he is being menaced, and subsequently my opinion was on his
15 behavior, i.e, to me.
16      If he could do this to an adult and showing no disrespect,
17 and be in my face, what does he do to an adolescent that acts
18 out?  So I drew red flags in my head as to how he acts and his
19 personality.  That's the answer.
20      Q    So by the same token, when I flip someone off in
21 traffic, that also must mean that I must curse at my
22 fifteen-month old son?
23      A    If you -- I mean if you go ballistic and -- is that
24 what you're saying?
25      Q    Hey, I'm --
```

47

```
 1     A     That you go ballistic --

 2     Q     I'm going

 3     A     --in traffic?

 4     Q     -- with the same line of logic that you just stated.

 5 You said -- I -- To summarize, his interaction with you, you

 6 transposed on what his interaction must be like with the

 7 children though you've never actually observed that.

 8     A     If you show road rage when you have a ten ton car or

 9 pickup truck in your hand towards another driver, that gives me

10 an opinion of what type of a personality you may be.

11     Q     All right, then.

12     A     The answer is yes.  Road -- It's called road rage.

13     Q     Okay.  Now you are relying on all of your opinions and

14 the newest of those opinions would have been from -- let me make

15 sure -- from May 2nd of 2014; correct?

16     A     No.

17     Q     Okay.

18     A     The answer is no.

19     Q     And you spent 20 hours as you testified to observe Ms.

20 ████ s parenting style to base your opinion; correct?

21     A     No.

22     Q     Now --

23     A     There were --

24     Q     If I

25     A     -- many --
```

                                                            48

        1   Q   -- need the --

        2   A   -- many other things.

        3   Q   -- court reporter to read back what your statement or

        4 the question was. It was specifically you observed her for over

        5 20 hours.

        6   A   I believe so. I could give you the exact amount if I

        7 could review the reports.

        8   Q   And so from that time -- And you observed her in

        9 isolation?

       10   A   What do you mean, in -- in a room by herself? Is that

       11 isolation?

       12   Q   Yes.

       13   A   No, I didn't observe her in a room by herself. I

       14 spoke to her.

       15   Q   It was just you and her?

       16   A   At certain times. Many times it wasn't.

       17   Q   And when it wasn't, who was there?

       18   A   ████ -- ████ I was observing when ████ was

       19 around. I spent a great deal of time for numerous reasons with

       20 Ms. ████ so if she was trying to con me or do defense

       21 mechanisms I would be able to get a good feel of what she is.

       22 So I based my opinion on the observation of Ms. ████

       23   I didn't see any psychotic or acting out behavior. I spoke

       24 in depth to her mother. I spoke in depth to her aunt. I had

       25 dinner with ████ and saw how he acted, how he picked up the

                                                                    49

```
 1  fork and knife.  I saw what she was doing to train him.  I did

 2  an intensive analysis like you tried to do with me.  What is the

 3  last book you read?  What is your work on this?  And -- and I

 4  read the court records, and I observed what was going on, and I

 5  got a good opinion of how she interacts; however --

 6       Q    And, sir, I --

 7       A    I have more to say.

 8       Q    I understand, but I don't even necessarily know if you

 9  are answering my specific question to you.

10       A    The answer is that I did see her in isolation a number

11  of times, a number of hours, and I saw her with her family --

12  trained in family therapy -- and I saw her with ███████ and I saw

13  her dimensionally at a baseball game when she was sitting about

14  75 yards from ████████, and I was sitting in the car, and I saw

15  her when the pictures were taken where ████████ with his

16  girlfriend -- now I should say estranged girlfriend or fiancée,

17  depending on what period of time what you would call her -- was

18  taking pictures and how some of the other women associated with

19  ████ --

20       'Q    And that --

21       A    -- treated --

22       Q    -- was in 2014?

23       A    -- ████████.  What?

24       Q    And that was in 2014.

25       A    I spoke to -- I spoke to the children.  I spoke to one

                                                              50
```

1 of my associates, Karen Wagner, and I spoke to Ms. ██████ --

2   Q   In --

3   A   -- and that's what I did.

4   Q   -- 2014?

5   A   Yes.

6   Q   And so you're basing all of your opinions on your

7 observations of a boy who was seven -- and is now nine years old

8 -- at the time and another boy who was fourteen, now sixteen

9 years old?

10   A   Could I be very clear. The answer is no. I am basing

11 upon the dynamics that happened with Ms. Wagner, a trained

12 evaluator and consultant. I'm basing it upon my conversations

13 with them. I'm basing it upon certain issues that happened

14 during the period of time. I'm basing it on facts on the

15 record, and with that -- it's not perfect. I don't have a

16 crystal ball.

17   I get a good probability that ██████ has been alienated.

18 He is -- he's acting out now. He needs therapy. ██████ is

19 totally in love with the mother. I don't believe he changed,

20 and there was alienation during the periods of the 14th through

21 the 15th -- the end of the 15th, and the mother is a good mother.

22 And subsequently I am not basing an analysis of ██████ but some

23 of his behavior was over the top when I was involved.

24   Q   How much do you get --

25   A   I think that --

```
 1     Q    -- paid for your --

 2     A    -- answers your question.

 3     Q    -- expert opinion?

 4     A    What?

 5     Q    How much do you get paid for your expert testimony?

 6     A    Today?

 7     Q    No.  I'm asking you, how much do you charge for expert

 8 testimony?

 9     A    It's -- it's a sliding scale.

10     Q    Okay.  So what's the highest hourly rate that you

11 charge for expert testimony?

12     A    I don't go by hours.  I go by day.

13     Q    Okay.  What's your highest per diem?

14     A    Are you saying -- You mean for this case?

15     Q    No.  I'm asking you, sir, what is the highest --

16          MS. ██████    Objection.

17 BY MS. ██████:

18     Q    You just said you have a sliding scale.

19     A    Right.

20     Q    What is the highest per diem that you charge to

21 testify?

22          MS. ████    Objection.

23          THE COURT:  What is the objection?

24          MS. ████    What does the price of his salary have to

25     do with the custody of my boys?
```
                                                                    52

```
 1          THE COURT:  All right.  The objection is relevance.

 2          MS. ██████████  Yes.  And ultimately, Your Honor, it

 3      is relevant to know how much he charges, if -- and if he

 4      has been -- if he has been charged, and Ms. ██████████ or Ms.

 5      ██████ is paying him, and/or if they're - if she hasn't paid

 6      him, what is the reason for that?

 7          THE COURT:  Overruled.  Go ahead.

 8          DR. WEINSTEIN:  Ms. ██████ paid me for my --

 9  BY MS. ██████████  (Resuming)

10      Q    No, no.  That wasn't my question.  My question was

11  what is the highest amount that you have charged for per diem to

12  testify as an expert witness?

13      A    You mean in any case?

14      Q    Yes.

15      A    Approximately 8000.

16      Q    And on the lesser side, how much charging -- what's

17  the least amount of per diem that you have charged a client?

18      A    Zero.

19      Q    How much have you charged Ms. ██████ to be here today?

20      A    $2000.

21      Q    Okay.  And when was that paid?

22      A    Ten days ago.

23      Q    And then after that was paid is when you had your

24  telephone conversations with the boys?

25      A    No.  Actually, I spoke to the boys before it was paid.
                                                              53
```

```
 1      Q    How many days before?

 2      A    It was like hours before.

 3      Q    Okay.

 4           MS. ██████████      No further questions, Your Honor.

 5           THE COURT:  All right.  Can this gentleman be excused?

 6           MS. ██████    Just one more question.

 7           THE COURT:  Go ahead.

 8                              -  -  -

 9                        REDIRECT EXAMINATION

10  BY MS. ██████

11      Q    Can you -- Dr. Monty, can you give us your account of

12  what happened at the baseball field?

13      A    What happened at the baseball field is that I said I'd

14  like to observe ██████ in a comfortable atmosphere.  He's a

15  great baseball player I heard, which I saw.  He is.  And how

16  everyone reacts, including you, in terms of ██████

17      And my reaction was I was threatened.  ████ was in my face.

18  I was told to leave, and I was told to stay away from his

19  children even though I wasn't near his children.  I was there

20  mainly, because I wasn't sure if I was going to testify for you

21  or not, to give you feedback in the best way to deal with a

22  contentious divorce.

23      And so I felt menaced.  That's my reaction.

24      Q    Okay.  And how long have you been working on this case

25  -- observing this case, working on this case?

                                                            54
```

```
 1    A    Three years.

 2    Q    Thank you.

 3         MS. ███████  One last follow up to that.

 4                        - - -

 5                  REROSS EXAMINATION

 6 BY MS. ███████

 7    Q    How much have you been paid in the course of three

 8 years working on this case?

 9    A    Maybe 12,000.

10    Q    Okay.

11         MS ███████  No further questions.

12         THE COURT:  All right.  Thank you, Doctor.

13         THE WITNESS:  Thank you.

14              ·              - - -

15         (Whereupon, the witness stepped down from the witness

16    stand.)

17                        - - -

18         (Whereupon, the excerpt testimony concluded.)

19                        - - -

20 //

21 //

22 //

23 //

24 //

25 //
                                                        55
```

COBB COUNTY

GEORGIA

2010

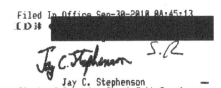

Filed In Office Sep-30-2010 0A:45:13
I D #

Jay C. Stephenson   S.R.
Jay C. Stephenson
Clerk of Superior Court Cobb County

IN THE SUPERIOR COURT OF COBB COUNTY

STATE OF GEORGIA

Plaintiff,	:	
	:	
	:	**CIVIL ACTION**
-vs-	:	
	:	**FILE NO.**
	:	
	:	
Defendant.	:	

FILED IN COURT
THIS *September 29* 20 10
AT_____M
JAY C. STEPHENSON
CLERK SUPERIOR COURT
COBB COUNTY, GEORGIA

ORDER

The above-styled matter having come before this Court for a final hearing on

September 17, 2010, on a *Complaint for Modification of Child Custody* filed by the

Plaintiff against the Defendant, seeking to be designated as primary custodial parent of

the parties' minor child, ▮▮▮▮▮▮▮▮▮▮▮▮▮▮▮ born ▮▮▮▮

▮▮▮ based upon substantial changes having occurred since the issuance of a Final

Order entered by the Court on February 20, 2008; and the Defendant having been served

and having retained counsel and having filed Responsive Pleadings; and each side having

presented evidence at the time of trial in the form of documents and testimony from the

parties and their respective witnesses; and the Court having considered all evidence

presented as well as the testimony of the parties and witnesses; and having further

considered and observed the demeanor and credibility of all said witnesses; and having

further considered the oral arguments of counsel as well as the; and the Court having also

considered the evidence in concert with the existing statutory and case law;

FROM THE MOB TO THE THERAPIST'S CHAIR

NOW THEREFORE, the Court makes the following Findings of Fact:

FINDINGS OF FACT

1.

The Defendant, ▓▓▓▓▓▓▓▓▓▓ became the sole legal and physical custodial parent of the minor child, ▓▓▓▓▓▓ (born February 2, 1999)) on February 20, 2010 in civil action file number ▓▓▓▓▓▓

2.

The Court finds that since the entry of the Court's Order on February 20, 2008, Mother/Plaintiff, ▓▓▓▓▓▓, has successfully completed this Court's requirements for drug and alcohol assessment and counseling, which was reported to the court by written letter from Diane Kee, MS, RN, CS in accordance with this Court's requirements.

3.

The Court finds that since the entry of the Court's Order on February 20, 2008, the visitation allowances of the Mother/Plaintiff (as directed by this Court) were exercised for a period of six (6) months under the supervision and observation provided by and through Wagner Consulting Services, ▓▓▓▓▓▓▓▓ Marietta, Georgia 30062. The supervision and monitoring provided by Wagner Consulting Service, included visitations supervised, monitored, and observed personally by Karen Wagner of Wagner Consulting Services. During such times, Plaintiff/Mother was fully, cooperative and compliant with the requirements of this Court's Order in this regard.

4.

Since the entry of this Court's Order on February 20, 2008, the Plaintiff purchased a home located at ▓▓▓▓▓▓▓▓ Georgia 30062 in which she resides, together with the child during her visitation periods.

5.

The Court also finds that since the entry of the Court's Order on February 20, 2008, the Plaintiff has made frequent requests to the Defendant to be able to have time with and access to the minor child, ██████████ in addition to that specifically outlined in the Court's Order of February 20, 2008, including times on the birthdays of ████████ notification of school events involving the child, Mother's Days, as well as requests to pick the child up for visitation times earlier to which the Plaintiff's requests were denied and additional times rarely considered by the Defendant.

6.

The Court further finds that since the entry of this Court's Order on February 20, 2008, the Plaintiff has been active in volunteer activities including, Boys and Girls Club of America, Women In Technology International for Digi-Girlz (an outreach program for middle school girls), elementary school classroom training in Junior Achievement Program, Year-Up (a mentoring program for underprivileged/at risk kids), and has completed the course, GaCSI (Georgia Cybersafety Initiative) designed by the GBI to help inform and guide Parents on how to keep child safe online as well as having completed a course on co-parenting of children in multiple homes.

7.

Since the entry of the Court's Order on February 20, 2008, the Defendant, ███ ███████, has sought and secured the services of persons other than the Plaintiff/Mother to keep, supervise or tend to ██████ in his absence without inquiring into the availability of the Plaintiff/Mother.

8.

Dr. Monty N. Weinstein, PSYD, appeared as a witness on behalf of the Plaintiff and was qualified as an expert in family therapy and psychotherapy with emphasis on custodial disputes, parenting time, family disputes and Parental Alienation Syndrome (P.A.S.), having appeared as an expert witness in over 2,000 cases.

9.

Dr. Weinstein testified that he had an intensive family therapeutic relationship with the Plaintiff during the past 2 years, to assist her in navigating through the situation involving the loss of custody of her two children.

10.

Dr. Weinstein further testified that in his professional capacity he met with the Plaintiff on 43 occasions, read and reviewed the trial transcript, reviewed email transmissions between the parties, engaged the Plaintiff in intense discussions and therapy about all conduct issues noted in the Court's Order of February 20, 2008 and made continued observations of the Plaintiff's demeanor, body language, state of mind, temperament and parenting skills. Dr. Weinstein also read and reviewed the deposition transcript of the Defendant ███████████ taken on September 1, 2010 and, further, observed Plaintiff's interactions and relationships with her children and observing the children's interaction and involvement with her during their times together. Dr. Weinstein also met with Karen Wagner as to her professional impressions in this case.

11.

Dr. Weinstein acknowledged that his observations and presence were obviously known by the Plaintiff but testified that, given the number of hours and occasions he was involved in his observations, the Plaintiff was sincere and genuine in her interactions with the child.

12.

Dr. Weinstein concluded that in his intense therapy with and observations of the Plaintiff, he did not see signs of a personality disorder and noted that the Plaintiff's focus was on the children.

13.

Dr. Weinstein testified Plaintiff was a fine and sensitive woman and a fit parent who should have a custodial role in the lives of her children.

14.

This Court further finds that Karen Wagner, BA, MS, Wagner Consulting Services, LLC, appeared as a witness on behalf of the Plaintiff and qualified as an expert in the field of Risk & Resiliency, Children at Risk, and Parenting Consultation.

15.

Ms. Wagner testified that her company, Wagner Consulting Services, was retained by the Defendant to provide supervised visitations and monitoring in accordance with the Court's Order of February 20, 2008.

16.

Ms. Wagner stated that she met with ████████████████████████ and reviewed the Court's Order prior to beginning her company's supervision of visitation between the Plaintiff and the minor child.

17.

Ms. Wagner testified that during the times she personally supervised the visitations between the Plaintiff and the child she never saw or heard anything occurring between the Plaintiff and the child that was contrary to the court's order or that was improper or inappropriate.

18.

Ms. Wagner further testified that, several months after the supervised visitation had been concluded, she was retained by the Plaintiff to observe and evaluate the progress of her children since the supervised visitation ended. In this regard, Ms. Wagner met with the children individually and together on 2 separate occasions, the last such occasion being in July, 2010.

19.

The Court finds that Karen Wagner described the Plaintiff's relationship with ████ as being very close. She stated that she observed nothing during the monitored visitation or during her subsequent relationship with and observation of the Plaintiff and children as a Family Consultant that would prompt this court to have any concerns about the well-being and safety of ████ in Plaintiff's care or about Plaintiff's ability to parent the child.

20.

Defendant testified that ████████████████████ spend approximately 4-6 hours each week together, except for the times they are with Plaintiff/Mother.

21.

Karen Wagner testified further that, based upon her observations, she believes Plaintiff would foster a strong relationship to exist between the child and both parents.

22.

The Court finds that the ▇▇▇▇▇▇▇ has requested additional time with her

mom directly to her father, this Court's Defendant. The Defendant responded that he

wanted to stick to the Court's Order.

23.

The Court finds that the Defendant regularly relies on ▇▇▇▇▇ and his family

to assist him when he cannot be with the child but does not call or seek to contact the

Plaintiff on such occasions.

24.

The Court finds that the minor child has reached her pubescent years and has

sought her mother's advice and involvement regarding those physical changes in her

being.

25.

The Court finds that the Defendant has created an environment where the child

expresses regular annoyance and frustrations with the Defendant's refusal to allow her

more time with her mom.

26.

This Court finds the Plaintiff to be fit and proper and duly qualified to serve as a

role model and parent to the minor child.

27.

The Plaintiff testified that she recognizes the importance of parental participation

and, as primary custodian of ▇▇▇▇ would never seek to minimize the Defendant's role

in ▇▇▇▇ ife and would always encourage mutual cooperation and participation in the life of the child.

28.

Plaintiff's hours are flexible and accommodating to be present for the child after school and accommodating to be with and prepare the child for school on weekday mornings.

29.

The Court finds that the Plaintiff/Mother is gainfully employed as an independent contractor capacity providing Technical Computer services to corporate concerns and, although future contracts with such entities are not certain, she has average gross earnings during 2008, 2009 and thus far in 2010 of $9,682.38 per month.

30.

That the Defendant is self-employed and reports gross monthly earnings of approximately $3,386.00 per month. This income includes monthly rent from a boarder who rents the finished basement of the Defendant's home.

CONCLUSIONS

1.

Since the issuance of the Court's Order on February 20, 2008 this Court concludes that there have been significant changes in the circumstances of the parents that directly affect and surround the minor child as outlined in the above Findings of this Court, which also include:

(1)   Plaintiff/Mother's mother's changes in her employment that will allow her accommodating and flexible time periods to provide care, guidance, and supervision of the child.

(2)   Plaintiff/Mother's strict compliance with and adherence to the specific requirements of this Court's previous conditions/restrictions.

(3) Plaintiff/Mother's change of residence and purchase of a 4 bedroom, 2 ½ bath house and lot located at ████████████████████ Georgia 30062.

THE COURT CONCLUDES that the Plaintiff has made consistent efforts to be involved with the child and in her life.

The Court also concludes that the Plaintiff is a fit and proper parent and fully capable of providing custodial care and guidance to the minor child;

The Court further concludes that it is in the best interest of the minor child to have open and liberal access with and availability to both of her parents.

2.

A modification of the previous custody disposition is warranted by all the changed circumstances in matters surrounding and directly affecting the minor child, which have occurred since this Court's Order of February 20, 2008 and is in the best interest of the child.

3.

Plaintiff/Mother has demonstrated since the entry of this Court's Order on February 20, 2008, that she is a fit person to have custodial entitlements of the child and is able to provide a suitable and caring home for her.

4.

It is in the best interest of the minor child that her custody be modified as

FORSYTHE COUNTY GEORGIA

2007

IN THE SUPERIOR COURT OF FORSYTH COUNTY
STATE OF GEORGIA

)
)
)
            Plaintiff,)   CIVIL ACTION FILE
vs.   )
)
)
)
            Defendant.)

. . .

PROCEEDINGS BEFORE
HON. HUGH W. STONE

FORSYTH COUNTY COURTHOUSE
CUMMING, GEORGIA

SEPTEMBER 4, 2007

APPEARANCES OF COUNSEL:
    For the Plaintiff:

    For the Defendant:

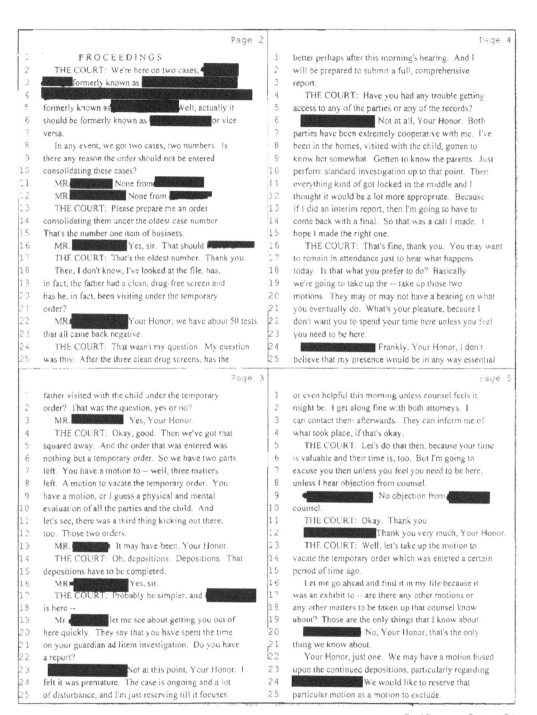

PROCEEDINGS

1   PROCEEDINGS
2   THE COURT: We're here on two cases, ▓▓▓▓▓▓
3 ▓▓▓▓▓▓ formerly known as ▓▓▓▓▓▓▓▓▓▓▓▓
4 ▓▓▓▓▓▓▓▓▓▓▓▓▓▓▓▓▓▓▓▓▓▓▓▓▓▓▓▓▓▓
5 formerly known as ▓▓▓▓▓▓▓▓ Well, actually it
6 should be formerly known as ▓▓▓▓▓▓▓ or vice
7 versa.
8   In any event, we got two cases, two numbers. Is
9 there any reason the order should not be entered
10 consolidating these cases?
11   MR. ▓▓▓▓ None from ▓▓▓▓
12   MR. ▓▓▓▓ None from ▓▓▓▓
13   THE COURT: Please prepare me an order
14 consolidating them under the oldest case number.
15 That's the number one item of business.
16   MR. ▓▓▓▓ Yes, sir. That should ▓▓▓▓▓▓
17   THE COURT: That's the oldest number. Thank you.
18   Then, I don't know, I've looked at the file, has,
19 in fact, the father had a clean, drug-free screen and
20 has he, in fact, been visiting under the temporary
21 order?
22   MR. ▓▓▓▓▓▓ Your Honor, we have about 50 tests
23 that all came back negative.
24   THE COURT: That wasn't my question. My question
25 was this: After the three clean drug screens, has the

1 father visited with the child under the temporary
2 order? That was the question, yes or no?
3   MR. ▓▓▓▓ Yes, Your Honor.
4   THE COURT: Okay, good. Then we've got that
5 squared away. And the order that was entered was
6 nothing but a temporary order. So we have two parts
7 left. You have a motion to -- well, three matters
8 left. A motion to vacate the temporary order. You
9 have a motion, or I guess a physical and mental
10 evaluation of all the parties and the child. And
11 let's see, there was a third thing kicking out there,
12 too. Those two orders.
13   MR. ▓▓▓▓ It may have been, Your Honor.
14   THE COURT: Oh, depositions. Depositions. That
15 depositions have to be completed.
16   MR. ▓▓▓▓ Yes, sir.
17   THE COURT: Probably be simpler, and ▓▓▓▓▓▓
18 is here --
19   Mr. ▓▓▓▓ let me see about getting you out of
20 here quickly. They say that you have spent the time
21 on your guardian ad litem investigation. Do you have
22 a report?
23   ▓▓▓▓▓▓ Not at this point, Your Honor. I
24 felt it was premature. The case is ongoing and a lot
25 of disturbance, and I'm just reserving till it focuses

1 better perhaps after this morning's hearing. And I
2 will be prepared to submit a full, comprehensive
3 report.
4   THE COURT: Have you had any trouble getting
5 access to any of the parties or any of the records?
6   ▓▓▓▓▓▓ Not at all, Your Honor. Both
7 parties have been extremely cooperative with me. I've
8 been in the homes, visited with the child, gotten to
9 know her somewhat. Gotten to know the parents. Just
10 perform standard investigation up to that point. Then
11 everything kind of got locked in the middle and I
12 thought it would be a lot more appropriate. Because
13 if I did an interim report, then I'm going to have to
14 come back with a final. So that was a call I made. I
15 hope I made the right one.
16   THE COURT: That's fine, thank you. You may want
17 to remain in attendance just to hear what happens
18 today. Is that what you prefer to do? Basically
19 we're going to take up the -- take up those two
20 motions. They may or may not have a bearing on what
21 you eventually do. What's your pleasure, because I
22 don't want you to spend your time here unless you feel
23 you need to be here.
24   ▓▓▓▓▓▓ Frankly, Your Honor, I don't
25 believe that my presence would be in any way essential

1 or even helpful this morning unless counsel feels it
2 might be. I get along fine with both attorneys. I
3 can contact them afterwards. They can inform me of
4 what took place, if that's okay.
5   THE COURT: Let's do that then, because your time
6 is valuable and their time is, too. But I'm going to
7 excuse you then unless you feel you need to be here,
8 unless I hear objection from counsel.
9   ▓▓▓▓▓▓ No objection from ▓▓▓▓
10 counsel.
11   THE COURT: Okay. Thank you.
12   ▓▓▓▓▓▓ Thank you very much, Your Honor.
13   THE COURT: Well, let's take up the motion to
14 vacate the temporary order which was entered a certain
15 period of time ago.
16   Let me go ahead and find it in my file because it
17 was an exhibit to -- are there any other motions or
18 any other matters to be taken up that counsel know
19 about? Those are the only things that I know about.
20   ▓▓▓▓▓▓ No, Your Honor, that's the only
21 thing we know about.
22   Your Honor, just one. We may have a motion based
23 upon the continued depositions, particularly regarding
24 ▓▓▓▓▓▓ We would like to reserve that
25 particular motion as a motion to exclude.

2 (Pages 2 to 5)

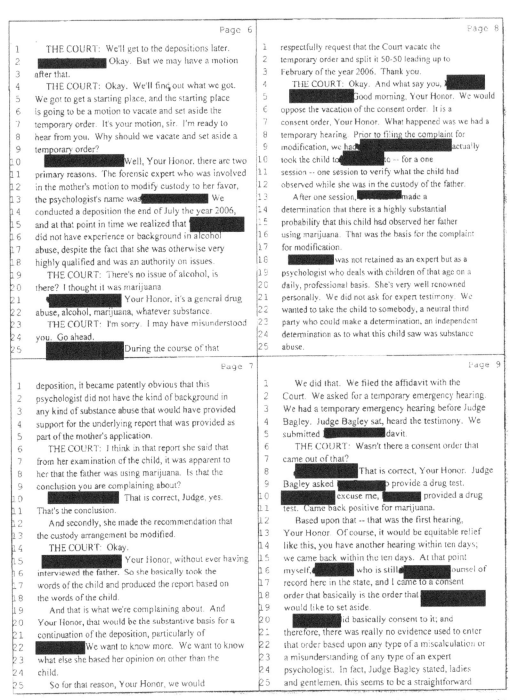

1   THE COURT: We'll get to the depositions later.

2   █████████ Okay. But we may have a motion

3 after that.

4   THE COURT: Okay. We'll find out what we got.

5 We got to get a starting place, and the starting place

6 is going to be a motion to vacate and set aside the

7 temporary order. It's your motion, sir. I'm ready to

8 hear from you. Why should we vacate and set aside a

9 temporary order?

10   █████████ Well, Your Honor, there are two

11 primary reasons. The forensic expert who was involved

12 in the mother's motion to modify custody to her favor,

13 the psychologist's name was ████████████ We

14 conducted a deposition the end of July the year 2006,

15 and at that point in time we realized that ████████

16 did not have experience or background in alcohol

17 abuse, despite the fact that she was otherwise very

18 highly qualified and was an authority on issues.

19   THE COURT: There's no issue of alcohol, is

20 there? I thought it was marijuana

21   █████████ Your Honor, it's a general drug

22 abuse, alcohol, marijuana, whatever substance.

23   THE COURT: I'm sorry. I may have misunderstood

24 you. Go ahead.

25   █████████ During the course of that

1 deposition, it became patently obvious that this

2 psychologist did not have the kind of background in

3 any kind of substance abuse that would have provided

4 support for the underlying report that was provided as

5 part of the mother's application.

6   THE COURT: I think in that report she said that

7 from her examination of the child, it was apparent to

8 her that the father was using marijuana. Is that the

9 conclusion you are complaining about?

10   █████████ That is correct, Judge, yes.

11 That's the conclusion.

12   And secondly, she made the recommendation that

13 the custody arrangement be modified.

14   THE COURT: Okay.

15   █████████ Your Honor, without ever having

16 interviewed the father. So she basically took the

17 words of the child and produced the report based on

18 the words of the child.

19   And that is what we're complaining about. And

20 Your Honor, that would be the substantive basis for a

21 continuation of the deposition, particularly of

22 ████████ We want to know more. We want to know

23 what else she based her opinion on other than the

24 child.

25   So for that reason, Your Honor, we would

1 respectfully request that the Court vacate the

2 temporary order and split it 50-50 leading up to

3 February of the year 2006. Thank you.

4   THE COURT: Okay. And what say you, ████████

5   █████████ Good morning, Your Honor. We would

6 oppose the vacation of the consent order. It is a

7 consent order, Your Honor. What happened was we had a

8 temporary hearing. Prior to filing the complaint for

9 modification, we had ██████████ actually

10 took the child to █████████ to -- for a one

11 session -- one session to verify what the child had

12 observed while she was in the custody of the father.

13   After one session, █████████ made a

14 determination that there is a highly substantial

15 probability that this child had observed her father

16 using marijuana. That was the basis for the complaint

17 for modification.

18   █████████ was not retained as an expert but as a

19 psychologist who deals with children of that age on a

20 daily, professional basis. She's very well renowned

21 personally. We did not ask for expert testimony. We

22 wanted to take the child to somebody, a neutral third

23 party who could make a determination, an independent

24 determination as to what this child saw was substance

25 abuse.

1   We did that. We filed the affidavit with the

2 Court. We asked for a temporary emergency hearing.

3 We had a temporary emergency hearing before Judge

4 Bagley. Judge Bagley sat, heard the testimony. We

5 submitted █████████ davit.

6   THE COURT: Wasn't there a consent order that

7 came out of that?

8   █████████ That is correct, Your Honor. Judge

9 Bagley asked █████████ provide a drug test.

10 █████████ excuse me, █████████ provided a drug

11 test. Came back positive for marijuana.

12   Based upon that -- that was the first hearing,

13 Your Honor. Of course, it would be equitable relief

14 like this, you have another hearing within ten days;

15 we came back within the ten days. At that point

16 myself, █████████ who is still █████████ ounsel of

17 record here in the state, and I came to a consent

18 order that basically is the order that █████████

19 would like to set aside.

20   █████████ id basically consent to it; and

21 therefore, there was really no evidence used to enter

22 that order based upon any type of a miscalculation or

23 a misunderstanding of any type of an expert

24 psychologist. In fact, Judge Bagley stated, ladies

25 and gentlemen, this seems to be a straightforward

3 (Pages 6 to 9)

1 case. From the record you can review that Judge
2 Bagley stated, I did not want this child brought
3 before a number of experts. I don't see any need for
4 experts in this case. ███████ has tested positive
5 for marijuana. He's going to deal with that issue
6 first and then we can move on from there.
7   So there is no legal basis or factual basis for
8 the Court to set aside a temporary order that Your
9 Honor --
10   THE COURT: A judge can set aside a temporary
11 order at any time basically for just about any reason
12 it finds appropriate. It's at his discretion.
13   ███████ Yes, sir. We would ask that you not
14 do that based upon the fact also that it's almost been
15 a year and a half and this child at this point would
16 be thrown back into the open water. She's finished
17 out almost a half a school year under that order,
18 started another one and now started another one. And
19 it's been -- I believe that was February of 2006 when
20 that order was entered, Your Honor.
21   We believe that it would not be in the best
22 interest of the child to throw out an order that's
23 been pending that long. And we'd ask you to deny that
24 motion.
25   THE COURT: All right. You have the last word.

1   ███████ Yes, Your Honor. To the best of
2 my understanding the counsel in this state, ███████
3 ███ was to sign a consent order. This was an order
4 entered based on a decision by the judge. On that
5 point, Your Honor, I simply --
6   THE COURT: I think it says it's a consent order.
7   ███████ Your Honor, what happened was the
8 judge -- ███████ Your Honor.
9 Judge Bagley heard about eight hours worth of
10 testimony at an emergency hearing. The other was
11 already set down for a temporary. We appeared at the
12 temporary. We did not see the judge going through all
13 the same evidence again, so we agreed on that one to
14 extend the original order of the court.
15   That's basically what they're referring to, a
16 consent temporary. It's -- you know, we came back in
17 here a week later and nothing had changed in a week.
18 There was no reason going forward and hearing all the
19 same evidence. So as into the -- using the word
20 consent, we did agree to consent to the original order
21 of the court, and the judge did hear evidence in that
22 from all the parties.
23   ███████ Judge, we had a pretrial conference
24 on that day in Judge Bagley's chambers with ███████
25 present. Based upon the judge's conferring with

1 counsel, we entered into a consent order regarding the
2 specific issue.
3   In fact, ███████ the only motion is an
4 emergency motion for modification of vacature of
5 consent order. So we agreed, ███████ and I, on
6 behalf of our clients, to consent to follow the
7 dictates of what that original order was. And we also
8 added some language to it as well, because there were
9 some issues regarding holiday and summer vacation and
10 things like that that we had to address that ███████
11 and I stood out in the hallway and tried to hammer out
12 on behalf of our parties.
13   So in all respect, it was a full agreement, the
14 parties were more than well apprised of the situation
15 at that particular time.
16   ███████ But then as the Court points out,
17 the Court can change the consent order. Consent does
18 not mean permanent and irrevocable. Consent simply
19 means what it means. That there was an agreement and
20 after the one week had passed. But not from the
21 original order. That was to the best of our
22 understanding at the time we wrote the motion.
23   The other thing, Your Honor, I wanted to address
24 is, I'm very surprised counsel mentions that ███████
25 ███ was quote, unquote, not an expert. She's an

1 expert. She's subject to testify --
2   THE COURT: That's really M-O-O-T. Your man
3 tested positive for marijuana. That's the basis to
4 move the child. Don't argue that to me. You are
5 wasting your time.
6   ███████ And, Your Honor --
7   THE COURT: This man voluntarily used marijuana,
8 a controlled substance, violation of the law in the
9 presence of the child. Based on -- she didn't say
10 that she was an expert in controlled substances. What
11 she said is based on an interview, and I'm qualified
12 to do an interview with the child, it appears to me
13 that he may be using it.
14   They came to court. He has tested. He's tested
15 as positive. You can't sit there and tell me there
16 was no basis for the temporary order. The temporary
17 order is by consent. If your client has a problem
18 with the order, it addresses itself to ███████ t
19 doesn't address itself any place else. He has the
20 advice of counsel. He tests positive for marijuana.
21 He's in court. He knows what he's facing. He agrees
22 to a consent order. There really is absolutely
23 nothing that is a basis to set aside that order.
24   Your man, who as you point out in other
25 affidavits, is most well educated, though he still

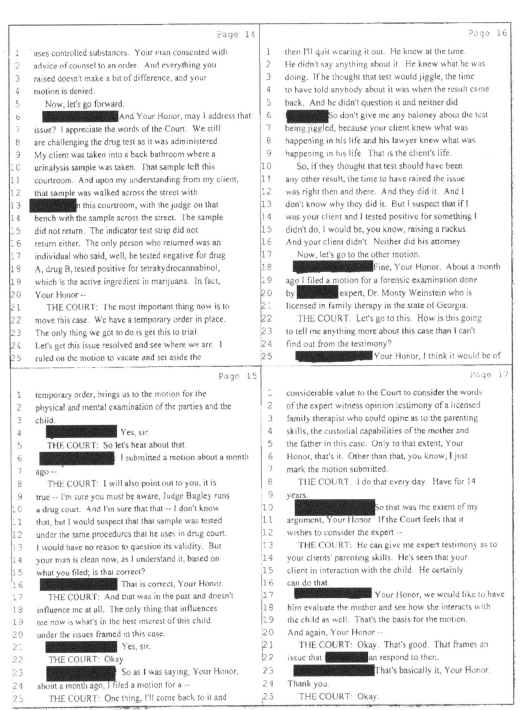

1 uses controlled substances. Your man consented with
2 advice of counsel to an order. And everything you
3 raised doesn't make a bit of difference, and your
4 motion is denied.
5 Now, let's go forward.
6 ███████████████ And Your Honor, may I address that
7 issue? I appreciate the words of the Court. We still
8 are challenging the drug test as it was administered.
9 My client was taken into a back bathroom where a
10 urinalysis sample was taken. That sample left this
11 courtroom. And upon my understanding from my client,
12 that sample was walked across the street with
13 ███████████ n this courtroom, with the judge on that
14 bench with the sample across the street. The sample
15 did not return. The indicator test strip did not
16 return either. The only person who returned was an
17 individual who said, well, he tested negative for drug
18 A, drug B, tested positive for tetrahydrocannabinol,
19 which is the active ingredient in marijuana. In fact,
20 Your Honor --
21 THE COURT: The most important thing now is to
22 move this case. We have a temporary order in place.
23 The only thing we got to do is get this to trial.
24 Let's get this issue resolved and see where we are. I
25 ruled on the motion to vacate and set aside the

1 temporary order, brings us to the motion for the
2 physical and mental examination of the parties and the
3 child.
4 ████████████ Yes, sir.
5 THE COURT: So let's hear about that.
6 ████████████ I submitted a motion about a month
7 ago --
8 THE COURT: I will also point out to you, it is
9 true -- I'm sure you must be aware, Judge Bagley runs
10 a drug court. And I'm sure that that -- I don't know
11 that, but I would suspect that that sample was tested
12 under the same procedures that he uses in drug court.
13 I would have no reason to question its validity. But
14 your man is clean now, as I understand it, based on
15 what you filed; is that correct?
16 ████████████ That is correct, Your Honor.
17 THE COURT: And that was in the past and doesn't
18 influence me at all. The only thing that influences
19 me now is what's in the best interest of this child
20 under the issues framed in this case.
21 ████████████ Yes, sir.
22 THE COURT: Okay.
23 ████████████ So as I was saying, Your Honor,
24 about a month ago, I filed a motion for a --
25 THE COURT: One thing, I'll come back to it and

1 then I'll quit wearing it out. He knew at the time.
2 He didn't say anything about it. He knew what he was
3 doing. If he thought that test would jiggle, the time
4 to have told anybody about it was when the result came
5 back. And he didn't question it and neither did
6 ████████ So don't give me any baloney about the test
7 being jiggled, because your client knew what was
8 happening in his life and his lawyer knew what was
9 happening in his life. That is the client's life.
10 So, if they thought that test should have been
11 any other result, the time to have raised the issue
12 was right then and there. And they did it. And I
13 don't know why they did it. But I suspect that if I
14 was your client and I tested positive for something I
15 didn't do, I would be, you know, raising a ruckus.
16 And your client didn't. Neither did his attorney.
17 Now, let's go to the other motion.
18 ████████ Fine, Your Honor. About a month
19 ago I filed a motion for a forensic examination done
20 by ████████ expert, Dr. Monty Weinstein who is
21 licensed in family therapy in the state of Georgia.
22 THE COURT: Let's go to this. How is this going
23 to tell me anything more about this case than I can't
24 find out from the testimony?
25 ████████████ Your Honor, I think it would be of

1 considerable value to the Court to consider the words
2 of the expert witness opinion testimony of a licensed
3 family therapist who could opine as to the parenting
4 skills, the custodial capabilities of the mother and
5 the father in this case. Only to that extent, Your
6 Honor, that's it. Other than that, you know, I just
7 mark the motion submitted.
8 THE COURT: I do that every day. Have for 14
9 years.
10 ████████████ So that was the extent of my
11 argument, Your Honor. If the Court feels that it
12 wishes to consider the expert --
13 THE COURT: He can give me expert testimony as to
14 your clients' parenting skills. He's seen that your
15 client in interaction with the child. He certainly
16 can do that.
17 ████████████ Your Honor, we would like to have
18 him evaluate the mother and see how she interacts with
19 the child as well. That's the basis for the motion.
20 And again, Your Honor --
21 THE COURT: Okay. That's good. That frames an
22 issue that ████████ an respond to then.
23 ████████████ That's basically it, Your Honor.
24 Thank you.
25 THE COURT: Okay.

5 (Pages 14 to 17)

FROM THE MOB TO THE THERAPIST'S CHAIR

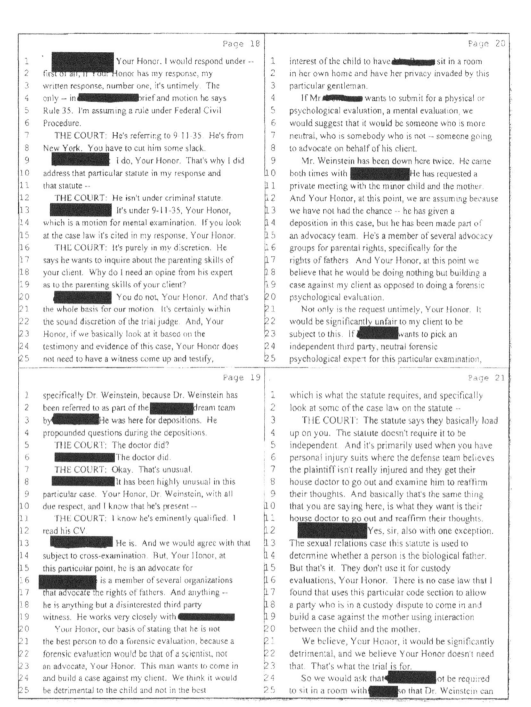

Page 18

1   ▮▮▮▮▮ Your Honor. I would respond under --
2   first of all, if Your Honor has my response, my
3   written response, number one, it's untimely. The
4   only -- in ▮▮▮▮ brief and motion he says
5   Rule 35. I'm assuming a rule under Federal Civil
6   Procedure.
7   THE COURT: He's referring to 9-11-35. He's from
8   New York. You have to cut him some slack.
9   ▮▮▮▮ I do, Your Honor. That's why I did
10 address that particular statute in my response and
11 that statute --
12 THE COURT: He isn't under criminal statute.
13 ▮▮▮▮ It's under 9-11-35, Your Honor,
14 which is a motion for mental examination. If you look
15 at the case law it's cited in my response, Your Honor.
16 THE COURT: It's purely in my discretion. He
17 says he wants to inquire about the parenting skills of
18 your client. Why do I need an opine from his expert
19 as to the parenting skills of your client?
20 ▮▮▮▮ You do not, Your Honor. And that's
21 the whole basis for our motion. It's certainly within
22 the sound discretion of the trial judge. And, Your
23 Honor, if we basically look at it based on the
24 testimony and evidence of this case, Your Honor does
25 not need to have a witness come up and testify,

Page 19

1   specifically Dr. Weinstein, because Dr. Weinstein has
2   been referred to as part of the ▮▮▮▮ dream team
3   by ▮▮▮▮ He was here for depositions. He
4   propounded questions during the depositions.
5   THE COURT: The doctor did?
6   ▮▮▮▮ The doctor did.
7   THE COURT: Okay. That's unusual.
8   ▮▮▮▮ It has been highly unusual in this
9   particular case, Your Honor, Dr. Weinstein, with all
10 due respect, and I know that he's present --
11 THE COURT: I know he's eminently qualified. I
12 read his CV.
13 ▮▮▮▮ He is. And we would agree with that
14 subject to cross-examination. But, Your Honor, at
15 this particular point, he is an advocate for
16 ▮▮▮▮ is a member of several organizations
17 that advocate the rights of fathers. And anything --
18 he is anything but a disinterested third party
19 witness. He works very closely with ▮▮▮▮
20 Your Honor, our basis of stating that he is not
21 the best person to do a forensic evaluation, because a
22 forensic evaluation would be that of a scientist, not
23 an advocate, Your Honor. This man wants to come in
24 and build a case against my client. We think it would
25 be detrimental to the child and not in the best

Page 20

1   interest of the child to have ▮▮▮▮ sit in a room
2   in her own home and have her privacy invaded by this
3   particular gentleman.
4   If Mr. ▮▮▮▮ wants to submit for a physical or
5   psychological evaluation, a mental evaluation, we
6   would suggest that it would be someone who is more
7   neutral, who is somebody who is not -- someone going
8   to advocate on behalf of his client.
9   Mr. Weinstein has been down here twice. He came
10 both times with ▮▮▮▮ He has requested a
11 private meeting with the minor child and the mother.
12 And Your Honor, at this point, we are assuming because
13 we have not had the chance -- he has given a
14 deposition in this case, but he has been made part of
15 an advocacy team. He's a member of several advocacy
16 groups for parental rights, specifically for the
17 rights of fathers. And Your Honor, at this point we
18 believe that he would be doing nothing but building a
19 case against my client as opposed to doing a forensic
20 psychological evaluation.
21 Not only is the request untimely, Your Honor. It
22 would be significantly unfair to my client to be
23 subject to this. If ▮▮▮▮ wants to pick an
24 independent third party, neutral forensic
25 psychological expert for this particular examination,

Page 21

1   which is what the statute requires, and specifically
2   look at some of the case law on the statute --
3   THE COURT: The statute says they basically load
4   up on you. The statute doesn't require it to be
5   independent. And it's primarily used when you have
6   personal injury suits where the defense team believes
7   the plaintiff isn't really injured and they get their
8   house doctor to go out and examine him to reaffirm
9   their thoughts. And basically that's the same thing
10 that you are saying here, is what they want is their
11 house doctor to go out and reaffirm their thoughts.
12 ▮▮▮▮ Yes, sir, also with one exception.
13 The sexual relations case this statute is used to
14 determine whether a person is the biological father.
15 But that's it. They don't use it for custody
16 evaluations, Your Honor. There is no case law that I
17 found that uses this particular code section to allow
18 a party who is in a custody dispute to come in and
19 build a case against the mother using interaction
20 between the child and the mother.
21 We believe, Your Honor, it would be significantly
22 detrimental, and we believe Your Honor doesn't need
23 that. That's what the trial is for.
24 So we would ask that ▮▮▮▮ ot be required
25 to sit in a room with ▮▮▮▮ so that Dr. Weinstein can

6 (Pages 18 to 21)

1 issue some type of a forensic opinion as to what he
2 believes. This case has been going on a year and a
3 half. He's going to watch them for 30 minutes or an
4 hour and then give -- that may more go to the weight
5 of the evidence, Your Honor, maybe not its
6 admissibility. But we don't believe it would be in
7 the best interest of this child to have to sit there.
8   We believe that the probative value for the court
9 is so limited as to this particular expert, because we
10 believe, Your Honor, that he is going to try to
11 advance a theory of parental alienation, and how he is
12 going to be able to do that and whether that is even
13 an acceptable thesis under the standard is a question
14 that remains for the Court. But is not one that would
15 need to have these people isolated with Dr. Weinstein.
16 And we would ask that the motion be denied.
17   THE COURT: And of course you have the last word,
18 sir.
19   Yes, Your Honor. Parental
20 alienation was never alleged in this case. The father
21 does enjoy visitation. But as far as the timeliness
22 of the motion goes, Your Honor, if we had had our
23 continued depositions at the end of September of the
24 year of '06, we would have been able to conduct an
25 inquiry of the mother, and we would have been able to

1 perhaps fashion a better, more detailed, more solid
2 motion to have her evaluated by our expert.
3   Unfortunately, depositions never took place.
4 Time passed, a lot of time passed, and I decided that
5 maybe we do need that psychological evaluation and
6 then do the depositions afterward.
7   So what I'm saying, Your Honor, is that there is
8 nothing that   did or that I did to protract
9 or extend the time of this case. We had depositions
10 in July that were called by mother's counsel and that
11 were not continued as was agreed upon at the last
12 deposition.
13   I do point out also, Your Honor, that Rule 35 is
14 a general civil section that should apply to any and
15 all civil practice anytime there's a mental or
16 physical examination that is needed, that the
17 appropriate forensic person be identified. A copy of
18 his CV be attached. We basically followed the
19 statute, Your Honor.
20   And one last thing I wanted to mention, dream
21 teams, I'm on several dream teams. I have a
22 handwriting expert in New York with whom I go to
23 Federal Court to uphold a dream team there. I have a
24 radiologist, a fellow named Dr. Tantliff in New York.
25 We're also called a dream team whenever we need to

1 debunk allegations on X-rays. And I do enjoy having
2 Dr. Weinstein on a case because of his fast and
3 substantial expertise.
4   All of these things, Your Honor, not
5 withstanding, I just leave it up to the Court to
6 decide whether to grant us the mental examination.
7 Thank you, sir.
8   Your Honor --
9   THE COURT: He will get the last word again. You
10 can talk as long as you want to. He gets to close.
11   Yes, sir. And I appreciate that.
12 Just one issue regarding depositions, Your Honor. We
13 had depositions scheduled last summer. We did agree
14 to continue them. The depositions went four days.
15 Three days, excuse me, Judge.
16   Two.
17   THE COURT: Two days.
18   And at that particular point, it was
19   that decided to go along at that point.
20 We agreed to continue it. I didn't hear anything from
21 his office for seven months to continue. At that
22 point, I requested a conference and I never got a
23 phone call back. That's the procedural nature of what
24 happened.
25   These depositions that   was supposed

1 to reschedule did not get rescheduled until 2007.
2 Your Honor, I had my depositions at that particular
3 point. And the reason why they went so long, and
4   comes in and says, well, you know, we
5 wanted to wait because it's untimely because we didn't
6 get the depositions rescheduled. Those depositions,
7 they've been rescheduled October, November, December.
8 They were not. I was noticed about three weeks at the
9 end of February, I had a trial calendar. If Your
10 Honor has seen the pleadings, you know the basic story
11 on that. So I just want to address the depositions.
12   Your Honor, with all due respect
13 to my very able opponent, I have a letter from
14   dated September 20th telling me he can't
15 make the continued depositions. I have a conflict
16 with scheduling on September 27th in the case of -- I
17 won't mention it on the record -- I therefore request
18 alternate dates in October regarding depositions. We
19 provided October, December dates. Busy, busy,
20 busy. And in February --
21   THE COURT: And you have the same problem with
22 your trial calendar. There are conflicts that come
23 up. He isn't necessarily hiding because he doesn't
24 control when a case gets on a calendar.
25   Your Honor, with all due respect

BROOKE COUNTY

WEST VIRGINIA

1998

IN THE CIRCUIT COURT OF BROOKE COUNTY, WEST VIRGINIA

███████████████, §

      Plaintiff/Respondent,

v.   §   ███████████████████████

███████████, §

      Defendant/Petitioner.   §

O R D E R

On the 20th and 21st days of January, 1998, came the defendant/petitioner herein, ███████████ hereinafter referred to as the "petitioner"), in his own proper person and by counsel, James P. Mazzone, Esq. and Jennifer S. Fahey, Esq., and as well came the plaintiff/respondent herein, ███████████████████ (hereinafter referred to as the "respondent"), in her own proper person and by her counsel, Lisa M. Bagay, Esq., to the matter set those days for a final custody hearing before the Honorable William F. Sinclair, Family Law Master for Brooke County, West Virginia, as to a *Petition to Change Custody* filed on the 10th day of October, 1996.

The Family Law Master for Brooke County, West Virginia has filed his *Notice of Recommended Order*. Upon the failure of either party to file objections and/or exceptions to said decision within ten (10) days ending on a day prescribed therein <u>or</u> subsequent to consideration of any such timely filed objections and/or exceptions, the Court does now make its decision.

(22) The petitioner would be a fit custodial parent based upon the uncontroverted testimony of Dr. Monty N. Weinstein, Dr. Charles William Hewitt, and both parties.

(23) In his written report to the Court (Petitioner/Defendant's Exhibit #3C), Dr. Charles William Hewitt states that "Mrs. Doyle, with characteristic lack of insight, projection, and sometimes outright misinformation, undermines ████ ███████" in his relationship with the subject child, ███████████ ███████

(24) Only those records specifically identified within his evaluation reports were reviewed and/or assisted in formulating Dr. Hewitt's opinions/conclusions.

(25) The State of West Virginia, Department of Health and Human Resources records (comprising Defendant/Petitioner's Exhibit #5 in this matter) are not listed within the "File Review" sections of the written reports rendered by Dr. Charles William Hewitt in this matter.

(26) By stipulation of the parties and the Guardian Ad Litem, Dr. Monty N. Weinstein, was qualified to testify in this matter as an expert and render opinions in the fields of Family Therapy, Abuse and Neglect, Sexual Abuse, Custodial Evaluations, Psychotherapy, Mental Health Administration and Clinical/Forensic Psychology. He is the director of the Family Therapy Institute, Brooklyn, New York.

(27) Dr. Monty N. Weinstein testified that he has expended approximately sixty (60) hours reviewing this case. He spent at

least two (2) weekends conducting an on-site "systems approach" analysis of ███████████████ s relationship with the petitioner, the petitioner's home, and the petitioner's various immediate and extended family members.

(28) The respondent testified that she refused to meet with Dr. Monty N. Weinstein "on advice of counsel". However, she was unable to testify as to why her counsel had so advised. Based solely upon a review of various records (including the extensive reports of Dr. Charles William Hewitt) and without benefit of any personal contact with the respondent, Dr. Weinstein concurred with Dr. Charles William Hewitt's psychological diagnosis of the respondent. However, he disagreed with Dr. Hewitt's conclusion that the respondent should keep and retain custody of the subject infant child, ██████████████ Dr. Weinstein testified that custody of ███████████████ should be placed in the petitioner herein for the following reasons, amongst others: the child would flourish in the petitioner's care and the petitioner would not undermine the relationship between the ████████████████ and the respondent. Dr. Monty N. Weinstein concurred with the results of a Minnesota Multiphasic Personality Inventory-2 performed by Dr. Charles William Hewitt on the respondent. Said test yielded a profile suggesting a naive and defensive attempt to present herself in a favorable light while tending to deny problems. She was determined to be not very introspective or insightful about her own behavior. In essence, Dr. Monty N. Weinstein believed the respondent to be in denial of her psychological condition. In

-10-

FROM THE MOB TO THE THERAPIST'S CHAIR

addition to the diagnoses of Dr. Charles William Hewitt, Dr. Monty N. Weinstein believes that the respondent may have an additional diagnosis of paranoia. However, upon examination by the Guardian Ad Litem, Dr. Charles William Hewitt intimated that Dr. Weinstein's lack of personal contact with the respondent rendered his conclusions somewhat suspect as they relate to the respondent such that they should be "confined to ███████████. To a reasonable degree of psychological certainty, it was Dr. Weinstein's opinion that the respondent is unfit to be the custodial parent of █████████ ██████████ He further testified that ███████████████ may begin to develop symptoms of fear, panic, anxiety, psychosomatic systems, and have no positive role model to emulate in the event that custody is not modified. Based upon extensive observations of the subject child and the petitioner, Dr. Weinstein witnessed no signs of anxiety or fear evidenced by the child to support Dr. Charles William Hewitt's concerns in the event of a modification of custody.

(29) As a result of his review of this case and based on his experience, training, education and background, Dr. Monty N. Weinstein testified to a reasonable degree of psychological certainty that:

> (a) a history of sexual abuse exists in the respondent's family and that ███████████'s step-sibling, ████████████ was sexually abused while he and the subject child were both in the respondent's custody;

-11-

(b) the respondent has personality disorders and/or manifests behavior which has and is undermining the petitioner's relationship with the subject child, ███████████████

(c) the respondent's personality disorders will cause irreparable damage to ████████████████████

(d) ██████████████████████ is exhibiting behavior consistent with the respondent's personality disorders and associated traits as well as the ongoing custody/ visitation disputes;

(e) the respondent is not fit to act as custodial parent;

(f) the petitioner is fit to act as custodial parent;

(g) custody of ████████████████████ should be transferred to the petitioner; and

(h) a transfer of custody to the petitioner will materially promote the welfare of ██████████ ██████, would be in said child's best interest, and will protect the child from the various and sundry dangers to which she is exposed while in respondent's custody.

(30) Dr. Monty N. Weinstein testified that any adjustment difficulties suffered by ██████████████████ upon a transfer of custody to the petitioner would be temporary in nature and/or capable of resolution through counseling. The Court finds Dr. Weinstein to be a very credible witness.

SPECIAL THANKS...

I'm not sure how I wound up with all this, but on the road, I made some great friends. One of those is Vickie Taylor, a paralegal, former journalist, and graduate of the University of Northern Colorado. Vickie is co-authoring this book and putting it into Kings English for me. She has helped me organize my thoughts. She has tried to keep me focused and on track. She has worked with me for the past seven years and has played an instrumental role in keeping Family Unity together and putting this book together. She has been a total support to me during this process, and especially during the past year when my eyesight has been causing me issues. She is a native of Colorado, living 45 minutes from the Rocky Mountains. My inner-city insanity along with her tranquil, mountain-air thoughts was a good combination. She has done brilliant work and extensive research for me, and during really busy times, she has helped keep me going.

I also worked with David Oles, Esq., for the past 15 years. He has been a good friend, an incredible attorney, and he deeply understands parental alienation. He is devoted to helping disenfranchised parents. He attended Harvard Law School, and is a wealth of information when I need legal assistance on difficult family law matters.

I have also worked for numerous years with Bruce Eden, a civil rights consultant who was a victim of the system, a friend of mine, and who wrote beautiful 1983 Federal Civil Rights Cases, and continues to write Amicus Curiae Briefs. He has been by my side on numerous cases, and we have achieved success for many of those clients together.

Karen Wagner has helped me with numerous cases and has traveled across the country with me to try to restore parenting time to alienated parents. Karen is a Harvard grad, and has dedicated her professional life to being an advocate for children.

Another dear friend of mine is Bobby Cahill. Bobby has worked by my side for many years. I was his expert and consultant. He has also been a devoted friend who was there for me whenever I needed him. He is an advocate, fighting for the rights of parents in high-conflict, family situations.

My dear friend James Wilks was instrumental in helping me co-found Fathers Rights Metro.

I would also like to thank and express my sincerest appreciation to Dr. Robert Polumbo, chief psychologist with the Archdiocese who has conducted brilliant psychological analysis for me in numerous cases while helping me navigate through many difficult and unusual cases.

Suzanne Silver has also worked numerous cases with me in terms of psychological insight, and has always been there by my side when I've needed her expertise and a second opinion.

My career has also been influenced by the brilliant mind of Dr. Seth Farber, who helped in terms of coercive psychiatry.

I would also like to express my gratitude to my dear friend and colleague, Robert Gould, now deceased, who was a brilliant psychiatrist. Gould worked with me on several cases, and his absence is deafening.

I am forever indebted to my dear friend and colleague Peter Lomtevas, who is an outstanding attorney. Peter helped me navigate through the judicial systems of several states. I have not seen him since the tragic death of his son. However, he has played a major role in defining parental alienation.

My psychology intern, Tina Jones, is currently training under my supervision, and she is doing outstanding work in aiding and assisting in family therapy. She is the future in the fight of parental alienation.

Another key player in my work and dear friend is Sonny Southerland, head of the People's Advocacy Group, whom I would like to thank for being a part of my team and standing up to the fight whenever I ask for his assistance. He is doing outstanding work as an advocate.

Special thanks to my dear friend Tom Shallow, who has worked by my side for many, many years, and who has selflessly dropped whatever he was doing to jump into a case and fight for the parental rights of total strangers.

Special thanks to my spiritual advisor and dear friend Father Anthony Cordona. Father Anthony is a former federal agent who is now a priest. He has totally been involved in my spiritual development for many, many years. When my sister died, he was by my side. My family is very close to his beautiful family and especially his daughter Katie, who has followed in his footsteps and is a New York City Police Officer.

My wife Kathy and I are forever indebted to the Honorable Jake Gold, Democratic District Leader in Brooklyn who played an instrumental role in his support of Kathy's election as a Supreme Court Justice. We thank Jake for his ongoing family support.

Following is a list of Dr. Monty Weinstein's peer-reviewed publications in annals of the American Psychotherapy Association, on the following topics: *Parental alienation, violence and terrorism, domestic violence and terrorism (International and National)*

The annals are the official magazine of the American Psychotherapy Association, www.Americanpsychotherapy.com

Psychotherapy in a Court Setting: The Dilemmas of Therapy in a Mandated Process, Published online Annals, The National Journal of The American Psychotherapy Association: March, 2016

Terrorism, Psychotherapy and the Clashing of Realities, Page 38, Spring 2007

Terrorism, the Psychological Dilemma, Page 50, Fall 2006

Terrorism and the Double Message, Page 44, August 2005

Terrorism and the Ongoing Phenomenon, Page 42, Spring 2004

Terrorism and Innocence, Page 44, Winter 2004

Terrorism and Dual Disasters, Page 42, Winter 2004

Three Years After 911, Page 45, Fall 2004

Terrorism and Our Children, Page 38, Spring 2003

Terrorism and the Double Standard, Page 50, Summer 2003

Terrorism and Inner Conflict, Page 43, Winter 2003

Terrorism, the Beginning Impact, Page 22, November 2002

Annals of Psychotherapy

Member Highlight April 2016

Member Highlight

We recently honored Dr. Monty Weinstein as our distinguished member highlight for April 2016

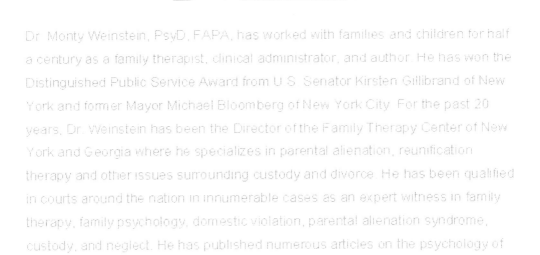

Dr. Monty Weinstein, PsyD, FAPA, has worked with families and children for half a century as a family therapist, clinical administrator, and author. He has won the Distinguished Public Service Award from U.S. Senator Kirsten Gillibrand of New York and former Mayor Michael Bloomberg of New York City. For the past 20 years, Dr. Weinstein has been the Director of the Family Therapy Center of New York and Georgia where he specializes in parental alienation, reunification therapy and other issues surrounding custody and divorce. He has been qualified in courts around the nation in innumerable cases as an expert witness in family therapy, family psychology, domestic violation, parental alienation syndrome, custody, and neglect. He has published numerous articles on the psychology of terrorism in Annals. Prior to being Director of the Family Therapy Institute, Dr. Weinstein served as the clinical director of numerous psychiatric facilities and he has also lectured on international affairs. His wife is an Acting Supreme Court Justice in Kings County, New York. He has five children and six grandchildren.

http://www.annalsofpsychotherapy.com/articles/2016/spring/memberhighlight.php

Dr. Monty, his wife the Honorable Katherine Levine, and daughters Moira and Sophia in England

Dr. Monty & wife Katherine Levine in the Hamptons

Dr. Monty, Moira, Sophia and wife Katherine Levine at the US Navy Yard in 2017.

Dr. Monty and wife Katherine Levine with the Torah at the US Navy Yard

Rabbi Joseph Potasnik, Katherine Levine, a survivor of a Nazi Concentration Camp and others at the Torah ceremony at the US Naval Yard

Moira, Lemore, daughter-in-law Karen and Sophia (Dr. Monty's daughters)

Dr. Monty and son Dr. Alan Weinstein

Dr. Monty & Family in Del Ray Beach

Son-in-law Dr. Michael O'Neal and Dr. Monty's friend Bobby Cahill

Robert "Bobby" Cahill and Dr. Monty

Dr. Monty's children: Sophia, Jacqueline, Alan, Moira and Lemore